ADVENTURES OF A WHITE-COLLAR MAN

Alfred P. Sloan, Jr.

ADVENTURES OF

A WHITE-COLLAR

MAN Alfred P. Sloan, Jr. 1875-

IN COLLABORATION WITH

BOYDEN SPARKES

New York   1941

DOUBLEDAY, DORAN & COMPANY, INC.

PRINTED AT THE *Country Life Press*, GARDEN CITY, N. Y., U. S. A.

Dedicated to

I. J. S.

My partner in the enterprise

Illustrations

Illustrations

Introduction

EVERY AMERICAN KNOWS that the General Motors Corporation is an extensive organization whose efficiency gives him, for some hundreds of dollars, a product which would be expected to cost many thousands and which, by some magic, is able to do this while still paying one of the highest of wage scales and yielding good dividends to its investors. We sometimes explain this magic by the phrases "Yankee ingenuity" or "American business enterprise." But we can be much more specific than this: the magic is really that of certain personalities and ideas, working in an environment which gave them scope.

Mr. Sloan's reminiscences give us a vivid and intimate picture of the most vigorous and productive era in American industry. They show how the human qualities of courage, faith, ability, consistency and very hard work can carry through to success despite difficulties or diversions. I find it hard to say whether I find this story more interesting as an interpretation of great corporate enterprise or as the personal story of a man who has heretofore been generally known only through his position and the end results of his work. But the chief message which this book brings to me—and I suspect that it was in Mr. Sloan's purpose to convey it—is the democratic and productive social philosophy that is implicit and also plainly stated throughout.

Emerson observed that an institution is the lengthened shadow of one man. In such a great industrial organization as General Motors, however, the lengthened shadow of this one man is merged with the shadows also of many other men—inventive mechanics, enterprising small businessmen, investors, and other curious fellows who had the urge and the courage to venture relatively enormous risks to find out what they could do, or to back their faith in an idea. The stamp of authenticity of these early craftsmen is found in the stains of oil and graphite in the letters which they wrote on their workbenches. Their little factories and shops, in the beginning as remote from each other as were farms in separate counties, were actually the first to feel, and then to recognize, that interdependence of one manufacturing unit upon another which is one of the chief characteristics of our modern technological age.

As the need for mutual reliance and collaboration became greater, the process of co-ordination moved from that of mere day-to-day co-operation to that of scientific planning, which tries to the best of its ability to forecast and to control its future along sound and constructive lines. Centralization of policy and co-ordination of control, which by setting related problems side by side made it possible to eliminate duplicate effort and dangerous divergency, was a major implement of this process of development. Another was standardization and interchangeability of parts, an advance which could not have been so readily effected under earlier communication methods in small, separate industrial units scattered over the country. It was these influences which underlay the boom days of Detroit—an episode in the history of the American industrial frontier fully as vivid, if not so colorfully dramatized, as the gold and oil rushes on geographical frontiers.

It is easier now to produce standard parts in factories widely separated; easier to maintain a steady flow of materials from these factories to focal assembling points so that the right quantities of the right units come to hand at the right time; easier thus to foresee the better balance of industry and the land, which Mr. Sloan rightly urges as of exceeding value to our economy. It is easier to do these things because of the work of those very industries themselves. Roads, vehicles, communication lines, reliable power—these are the requisite arteries for both the co-ordination and the distribution of manufacturing activity more widely through our land.

By word and example Mr. Sloan emphasizes the essential importance of the scientific management which had its origin in the co-ordinating work of the early industrial pioneers and which finds its greatest strength in the insistence upon "engineering care to get the facts" and the unprejudiced use of those facts. Essential also is that kind of free individual initiative which will undertake such scientific approach and planning with full recognition of the social implications involved; which will, as Mr. Sloan insists it must, broaden its social horizon and seek so far as it may to practice industrial statesmanship.

This story typifies an era of industrial growth such as may well again be repeated, given opportunity and a favorable environment. It recounts the history of a career based primarily upon those individual traits to which America has always given encouragement. The social-economic philosophy of Mr. Sloan as here expressed, while differing in some respects from that

Introduction

which from time to time has been in vogue, represents conviction as to the means by which the well being of workers, industry and the nation would be best served. And for this social philosophy it can be said that, as applied, it brought the desired results—expanded employment at relatively high wages, good profits and efficient service to the public—thus promoting the basis for higher living standards and a better life for all.

DR. KARL T. COMPTON
President, Massachusetts Institute of Technology

PART I

The First Adventure

I was seeking a position. That was the genteel phrase with which a young man went after a job in 1895. This was why I endured the embarrassed ages of waiting for the moment when I might be taken into the awesome presence of Mr. John E. Searles.

Others waited for a chance to see this busy man. I was sure the least among them had a better right than I to take his time. I was thin as a rail, young and unimpressive. I felt my mere presence was effrontery, for Mr. Searles was important. He was supreme in the American Sugar Refining Company. These were its general offices, crowded with people at desks. He had many other business interests. His home in Brooklyn was considered the most imposing in the city. He belonged to exclusive clubs, and his name was frequently in the newspapers. Who was I to take his time, even if my father did know him personally?

I tried my eyes against the dazzling centers of the steel-bluish arc lights overhead. The electrical lighting was about the only thing in those offices which made any sense to me. From the pencil-like cylinders of carbon sputtering with electric fire in one of the big glass globes I could follow the current, in fancy, clear to the powerhouse. After all, I was a bachelor of science in electricity, graduate of Massachusetts Institute of Technology. By keeping this encouraging fact to the forefront of my mind I kept my nerve, a little.

There was further comfort in the knowledge that my father had spoken about me to Mr. Searles; that would have been assurance enough for most. But I was shy by nature. Asking favors and pushing myself into places where I am a stranger always did go against my grain.

During my college years the country had been passing through the panic of 1893. Hungry men had crowded around the charity soup kitchens. Coxey's Army marched out of the West. While I waited on Mr. Searles, William Jennings Bryan was preaching that what the country needed to save it was cheaper money, specifically, free coinage of silver as well as gold at a ratio of sixteen to one. That did not make it any easier to find a job. My discouragement was stronger because I had worked so hard at college. As I look back, I believe it to be the most discouraging point of my whole life. I had been a grind. I had worked every possible minute, so that I might be graduated a year ahead, with the class of 1895.

However, instead of getting right after a job, following the summer vacation, I returned to college. I had been working on certain engineering projects with one of the professors, and an offer of a fellowship tempted me. The work we were doing was not important and nothing came of it. In consequence, it was late in 1895 before I really began to hunt for a place to work. Probably most young men are disturbed when first they pit themselves against the world. As I was naturally of a serious turn of mind, I suppose I was more than ordinarily troubled when I had failed to find work at any of the places where I applied. There must be many among the 150,000 college graduates of 1940 who will understand why my heart leaped when a mustached young man spoke: "Sloan? Mr. Searles will see you now, for just a minute."

Curiously, recollection of Mr. Searles' face has faded. But I remember his lean frame, his dark ministerial clothing, even my queer feeling of relief as he called me "Alfred." Of course, I was at ease as soon as we began to talk, for he and my father really were friends notwithstanding that Mr. Searles was a business giant. They were associated closely in Methodist Episcopal Church work in Brooklyn and had begun their acquaintance many years before in New Haven, where I was born.

What I got from Mr. Searles was a letter of introduction to a man in Newark, New Jersey. I have forgotten other details of my call, but later visits to his office taught me that it was rare to get more than a minute of uninterrupted conversation with Mr. Searles. He was habitually rushed; telephones rang and he could not resist answering; subordinates hurried into his presence, hurried out. He himself had frequent flashes of thought impelling him to action on matters seemingly more pressing than what was in hand. So I cannot believe he could have told me much about the small business he was backing over in New Jersey. I do know that before he gave me the letter he made sure I could make mechanical drawings. That was what he arranged for me—a job as draftsman.

The brownstone façade of No. 240 Garfield Place in Brooklyn looked like thousands of other houses standing in monotonous rows in New York. But I feel sure no other of those houses contained so much happiness as ours when I came home and told my good news. I was the eldest of five; four boys and a girl. There was excitement for us all in the fact that I had a job in the mechanical field, so that my education would count. From the time I was eleven and began attending Brooklyn Polytechnic Institute I had been interested in mechanics, in engineering.

So one of the Sloan children was launched. I know that at her end of the table my mother glowed; and father, after saying grace, carved the roast almost with a flourish. I do not mean to suggest that my prospect of a salary was responsible. Father certainly was not rich, but he had always managed to keep us in comfortable circumstances. As a rule, there was a cook in our kitchen, but if there were not, my mother well knew how to cook. She was the daughter of a Methodist Episcopal minister. Father was the son of a private-school master. Neither had any business forebears.

Well, I am bound to admit the first sight of my opportunity was disappointing. It was a gloomy, machinery-cluttered loft in a building in Market Street in Newark, tenanted by small and shabby manufacturing concerns. I worked there as a draftsman for several months, pending removal of the business to near-by Harrison. But that was even more disappointing. In all that industrial squalor was no hint that wonderful things were hidden there for me.

Not far from a city dump on a weed-grown, marshy plain was an old, weather-worn building, like an overgrown barn. In its indefinite yard there was a small mound of coal and a great mound of reddish-gray cinders and ashes; also a disorderly accumulation of discarded machinery of which I still seem to see one shape, the rusty cylinder of a worn-out steam boiler, all part of a junk yard next door. Once the factory had been painted brown. Only one word describes it: "dirty." Smoke from the dump carried an acrid odor. Eventually across the wall nearest the railroad track there was lettered in black this legend: HYATT ROLLER BEARING COMPANY.

I remember going inside where a small section set apart from the worst of the noise and dust of the shop had been divided into offices. But then there is a blank spot and I have to orient the rest of the experience from the table where I worked in the drafting room. I was the assistant of a jolly, intelligent fellow named Charles Lockwood, much older than I. He was the one who explained to me the importance of the device produced in that plant, the Hyatt flexible roller bearing. These were great friction reducers when installed in line shafting that had been turning on Babbitt-metal bearings. I remember Lockwood enjoyed talking about his long association with his par-

An American family of the 80's on summer vacation. The boy on the high-wheeled bicycle is Alfred P. Sloan, Jr.

*Alfred P. Sloan, Jr., in 1895, just out of M. I. T.
and "seeking a position."*

ticular hero, the inventor of the bearing, John Wesley Hyatt, who was also the inventor of celluloid.

This man Hyatt, with a very limited knowledge of scientific processes, had, in developing celluloid, really opened men's minds to the possibilities of the whole field of plastic materials. Today we have hundreds of these new materials, and we have just begun. But celluloid was the first.

The antifriction bearing put at the disposal of engineers a workable instrumentality of priceless value. Hyatt was a gifted, practical, hard-working inventor in a period when inventors were able to work with reasonable hope of producing something useful as individuals rather than as cogs of great research organizations.

The talent for invention has flourished in America as nowhere else, possibly because America in those days gave that talent the broadest opportunity. In small shops, in barns or attics, a host of American inventors down through the years have been able to accomplish remarkable things. But in our times a great change has occurred, not fully understood. Hereafter we are not likely to get inventions from individuals working as Mr. Hyatt worked, or as Charles F. Kettering worked when he developed his first electric automobile starter in a barn. I realize all this as I look back to the crude apparatus available to Mr. Hyatt and compare his little workshop with our modern research laboratories, such as that of General Motors. Today John Wesley Hyatt—and many inventors of his time—with all his accomplishments would find himself regarded as scientifically illiterate. As a matter of fact, he would be. The modern research laboratories of industry demand men having years of training in some form of science, whose talents can be coordinated on a specific problem. Today hundreds of thousands, and sometimes millions, of dollars are spent before the objective is reached, and there are more failures than successes. Hence for research progress we must look to the highly developed organizations maintained by large industrial units. Great resources are needed to cope with the complexities of the undiscovered.

Out of research our economy needs a continuous flow of new industries in order that we may advance our standard of living and also create additional employment. But that is not all. We must encourage technological progress whereby things currently useful may be produced at lower costs, hence distributed at lower selling prices, thus bringing them within the reach of a constantly increasing number. In other words, more things for more people in more places. Technological progress—and it is a pity more do not appreciate it—is the one sound approach to increased employment and higher wages. There is no other way. Irrespective of what is said to the contrary, new industries can be created, present industries can be expanded, unemployment can be eliminated in a practical way.

But rather than in Mr. Hyatt, the inventor, my interest at first had been captured by a tall young fellow in the adjoining office, the bookkeeper. He was a merry-eyed, rosy-cheeked Norwegian with an accent. In less than no time we were close friends. Before long we were to become partners.

The general manager at the Hyatt plant was a big Scandinavian with a great mustache. His name was Tellefsen, and he had been there only a year or so when I appeared in the drafting room. Previously, Tellefsen had been running a building-construction job in Buffalo. Peter Severin Steenstrup had been the paymaster on that same job. Tellefsen had invited Pete to come and be his bookkeeper soon after he was settled at the Hyatt plant.

I soon began to wonder how secure my job was. Literally, the business was being operated from week to week. Each payday was a crisis. The intensity of it was something to be gauged by the manner of Pete's return from the Manhattan office of Mr. Searles. Before he started out he would wave the envelope containing the pay roll. Invariably he'd say, "Well, if you fellows want to go on working, you better pray I'll find Mr. Searles in a good humor this morning." For months the gross business of the company had totaled only a few thousand dollars, but the pay roll and the other charges, for raw materials, freight and other things, had amounted to much more. The difference had always been supplied by Mr. Searles out of his own pocket. But Mr. Searles was becoming grumpier by the week, according to Pete. Consequently all of us, Mr. Tellefsen included, were relieved each time Pete returned bearing another check drawn against the Searles bank account.

Only the men in the shop were paid by the week. These included a foreman, several who ran the winding machines, a couple of brass finishers, and the man in charge of our power plant, who stoked his own fire under the boiler of our little ten-horsepower steam engine. The few office employees were paid by the month. I got fifty dollars. Pete got a little more. The secretary of the company was a man named Hudson. He had a desk in the office and was in charge of sales. In fact, he was the whole sales force of the Hyatt Roller Bearing Company. A bearded man, he had considerable dignity. Every boy in that time knew that ball bearings in bicycles and roller skates meant much greater speed and ease. You used a superlative when you said of anything that it was "ball-bearinged." But somehow our Mr. Hudson seemed unable to make businessmen understand that our flexible roller bearings would save money by doing for their machinery somewhat as ball bearings did for bicycles.

Without roller bearings or ball bearings, the modern automobile would be impossible in its present form. Our ability to concentrate heavy loads on small surfaces is what makes present designs possible. Indeed, much machinery of every character would become useless and would require redesign with reduced efficiency if you were to take away its ball or roller bearings. Nowadays, due to improved steels, astounding loads can be carried on the point of a ball —as in a ball bearing.

But I am talking about a period when men did not know how to make steel hard enough to support a heavy weight on a point of its surface or on a line of its surface, as is done by a roller when supporting a load. Roll a ball under your hand on a table and roll a pencil in the same manner. What you feel are "point" and "line" bearings. But to understand what mechanics mean by a surface "bearing," grasp a pencil in your hand and use your other hand to make it turn as a piece of shafting. Now, the lower half of the shaft is supported everywhere by contact with your hand—the upper half is not supported, merely covered. The advantages of ball and roller bearings were obvious many years ago to mechanical people. The difficulty was the weakness of existing metals. If only they could be made durable enough for machines heavier than bicycles. But there was a further difficulty almost invariably present, even when the loads were not too heavy, as in line shafting wherever power was being mechanically transmitted, or in cars used in coal mines. This other trouble was the crudity of machinery. Solid steel rollers, being inflexible, were not satisfactory at that stage, but a Hyatt flexible roller bearing was different. We had something. Our spirally wound tube roller had a springlike quality, yielded to irregularities caused by poor manufacture, thus making automatic adjustments between housing and bearing.

Even I succeeded in making a sale. Through my father I sold my first set of bearings to Bennett, Sloan and Company.

"Well," father said one night, "do you think I could save any money using these roller bearings in my business?"

I made some quick pencil sketches. One showed a roller unit. In an average installation, the rollers roughly resembled lead pencils, somewhat thicker and about as long, or longer. The basic operation in our plant was manufacturing these roller units. They were formed in winding machines. Strips of cold steel were turned spirally, and the tube thus formed was cut in sections of the proper roller length.

These rollers were arranged so as to form a jacket around shafting wherever it required support. They were held in this relationship by brass yokes and steel boxes designed to fit in the usual pillow boxes, or hangers, with which shafting was supported. Father knew what Bennett, Sloan and Company were spending for power, and I tried to explain to him how much was wasted through friction. Of course, for his business the saving was relatively unimportant.

Characteristically, although darkness had fallen, my father was still at his desk when I arrived at No. 100 Hudson Street, Manhattan, to survey his machinery and to close the deal. It was a small order—scarcely $150, as I recall it. We went upstairs where there were a few mixing machines in which different grades of coffee were blended, some coffee roasters and a belt conveyor. Father again questioned me about the savings in power and oil. He was careful of money. When he needed a new white collar, he would go into a store and buy one white collar.

Happily, I had facts, gathered from tests. The bearings would save enough to justify the investment. He signed the order.

I liked the Hyatt bookkeeper, Peter Steenstrup. In the old country he had gone to Latin college, learning several languages, but English was not one of them. We teased him when he made a mistake, but he was good-natured. During our lunch hour usually we went to Newark, a fifteen or twenty minute walk. So we fell into the habit of talking about the affairs of the Hyatt Roller Bearing Company. As boys will, we spoke our minds freely. We were sure we could run things better.

It so happened that Mr. Hudson had returned from Providence, Rhode Island, without an order on which the firm had counted heavily. Brown & Sharpe Manufacturing Co. were about the best-known makers of precision tools in the country. If they were to install our flexible roller bearings in their new shop, the fact would have an advertising value for our business. It was a bigger-than-average job and it would be the means of impressing every machine-shop owner in the United States that anti-friction bearings were not just a freakish innovation. Pete and I had grown careless in our criticism.

"I'd like a chance to go to Brown and Sharpe," boasted Pete. "I believe I could get that business."

John Wesley Hyatt invented celluloid, the first plastic, and the flexible roller bearing.

The Sloan families, father and son, in 1899. Mrs. Alfred P. Sloan, Jr., stands behind her husband at the left.

"What's that?" The boss had spoken in a sharp tone, and we were frightened.

"Oh, we were just talking."

"Talk's cheap! We can't have fresh guys around this plant. Since you're so smart, Steenstrup, you can go to Providence. Don't come back unless you get that order."

Poor Pete! An immigrant kid who couldn't speak English, except in broken phrases. That was the way Mr. Hudson spoke of him after his departure. The old gentleman's feelings had been hurt. But after five days' absence, Peter Steenstrup walked into the office, carrying his clumsy, old-country valise. He was back from Providence. Amazingly he had a signed order from Brown & Sharpe for a complete installation of Hyatt roller bearings.

The way Pete explained his success was that the one who had refused to give Mr. Hudson the order was a man about seventy who was just not interested in any newfangled scheme to make shop wheels turn more easily. So when Pete came along, after the matter had been settled, his temper was rasped. Pete said he was ordered out of the office when he became persistent. But Pete went back. He cried. He told the Brown & Sharpe man he was ruining his life, that he would lose his job. The old gentleman began to listen out of kindness, and Pete got the order. But the effect of Pete's success on our secretary and salesman, Mr. Hudson, was terrible. Tears came into his eyes, he was so chagrined. Much as I liked Pete, I felt pretty bad then, and worse when Mr. Hudson began to take his belongings out of his desk. He had resigned. The company was without a secretary, but before many months it was to be without a president as well.

The business was being operated badly. We seemed to capitalize only a fraction of our opportunities. Both Pete Steenstrup and I saw that plainly, but we could do little. I was troubled about it because I was impatient to get married. But how could I when I wasn't getting anywhere in business? It was just at this time that I met Lieut. William M. Wood, of the United States Navy. He was an Annapolis-trained man, considerably older than I. He seemed to spend all his time ashore working on some inventions.

He was trying to make a mechanical icebox twenty years ahead of his time. What brought him over to the Hyatt plant at Harrison was his need of some roller bearings for the all-important compressor of his refrigerating machine. Our first meeting was sometime before the Spanish-American War.

It is astonishing what you can do when you have a lot of energy, ambition and plenty of ignorance. Lieutenant Wood's immediate manufacturing proposition was for refrigerator boxes in apartment hotels and apartment houses. By a system of insulated, circulating pipes, all these boxes would be supplied with cold brine from a plant in the basement. I did not know a thing about electric refrigeration; I did not know much about Lieutenant Wood's mechanism. As I look back on it now, I can see that its cost alone made it impractical, but then I was a kid, infected with Lieutenant Wood's blind faith. He needed someone who could design a circulating system and he needed a sales manager. At a time when I felt the need of an escape, he offered me a job. Here was a handsomely uniformed rescuer who would get me off the Harrison dump.

I resigned from Hyatt and joined Lieutenant Wood over in Manhattan. Our office was No. 11 Broadway. But the factory had been established in Bridgeport, to be close to The Bullard Manufacturing Company. They made precision tools and had contracted to make Lieutenant Wood's compressors under his direction. His business was called the Hygienic Refrigerator Company. We didn't have much money.

My youthful belief in that enterprise astonishes me now. I do not think there was a hotel anywhere using a centrally controlled refrigerating plant to distribute "coldness" as we planned to do. The big ice plants in every city manufactured and distributed artificial ice. Hotels, ships and breweries had cold-storage plants. Of course, Lieutenant Wood's conception was possible. But was it practical? Now, in essence, the task of engineers is to make possible things practical. But my job was to find some customers.

Mark Rafalsky was operating in New York at that time as a builder. To my lasting surprise, he gave me a contract to install our system of refrigerators in two new apartment hotels. One was in 44th Street, between Fifth and Sixth avenues. The other was up near the American Museum of Natural History in Columbus Avenue. One of the backers of our company was a rich man in Boston, and through him we installed a unit in a hotel near the Copley-Plaza. The boxes worked! In fact, they functioned too well. I had put an excess of coil in some and they got too cold. They were only large enough to hold a little food and a few bottles. But they also provided running ice water. One or two of the circulating systems, I think, are still in service.

Mrs. Sloan and I were married that summer, 1898. She was Miss Irene Jackson, of Roxbury, Massachusetts. The way things looked, we could afford this step, but in a short time there was a jolt. Lieutenant Wood's machine failed us. In every case, his units had to be replaced. Then he died, and after a time the Hygienic Refrigerator Company was liquidated. I respected Lieutenant Wood then, and still do. He was an innovator, and without such people how many of our fine mechanisms would get a chance to begin their evolution? While I was with Lieutenant Wood there had been some interesting developments in the Hyatt Roller Bearing Company. Out of them came a chance for me, and for Peter Steenstrup too.

Mr. Searles had decided that he would put no more money into Hyatt. He declined to be its angel any longer. Unless some new backer could be found, it would be necessary to close down the works.

Because of the friendship of my father and Mr. Searles, they had discussed the situation, with the result that I went back to Hyatt. My father and a man named Donner, an associate of Mr. Searles in the American Sugar Refining Company, had bought into the company. I think Mr. Donner and my father each put up $2500. That was as far as Mr. Donner would go, but my father said he would advance more if the business showed any promise. Thereafter Pete, instead of going with the pay roll to Mr. Searles, went to my father. Pete and I had become partners.

When I went back, my salary was $175 a month. It seemed a lot of money to young Mr. and Mrs. Sloan. Possibly that is why I worked so hard. Pete and I scarcely ever stopped. We had six months to put the business on its feet, and we made good. With Pete selling and with me handling the production end, in our first six months we made a profit of $12,000. I'm not likely to forget that. Pete was given the title of sales manager. I was general manager.

My father made that investment on my account, but I would be unfair to myself if I did not also say that he did it because he was satisfied that I could get the Hyatt Roller Bearing Company on its feet.

On Sundays, Pete Steenstrup nearly always came for dinner. He was like a member of the family. Sunday nights, my father, Pete and I would talk and plan.

But for a long time after we had shown we could make money the business faced a crisis each Saturday. Pay-roll worry has whitened a lot of hair in this country, mine included. To spare my father, we had to get payment as soon as we made delivery of an order. A part of the excitement on a Saturday morning was in hunting through the mail for checks. Sometimes we needed as much as $150 or $200 more than we had. Father always obliged us. Nevertheless, it was a struggle for him and for us, and money was not available, except in small amounts. When a business is making money and expanding, it is to be expected that it will always be short of capital, simply because it is too successful in relation to its resources.

An ironical incident recurs to me now. I always

bought a New York paper at Jersey City in the evening on my way home, when I changed there from train to ferry. On a night when I was in an especially good humor due to some big order, I read a shocking thing. The banner headlines told of the business failure of John E. Searles.

Now, I want to say again that the business would have died had it not been for my father's willingness to risk his savings. Mr. Searles and he, in turn, carried it through what my friend, Charles Kettering, calls the shirt-losing zone. Yet my common sense makes me wonder if my father would take such a chance these days, when the attitude of Government has been so discouraging to men who might support a new business through its inevitable money-losing stages.

It seems to me that it is an illustration of what was then going on and what undoubtedly is still going on in the struggle for existence of many small units of business trying to develop some article or perform some service. The early history of several other parts of what now constitutes General Motors tells the same story. Yet see what has happened. These businesses now employ tens of thousands. They distribute millions of dollars in pay rolls directly, and indirectly many times as much. Right here lies a question very much before us—how to help small, inadequately financed units of business. The answer is not to be found in action by a paternalistic Government. What is needed is an adequate opportunity for hard work and intelligent management, based upon the principle of the survival of the fittest. Merit and initiative will find a way, given half a chance.

One day in our mail we found a letter from Ko-komo, Indiana. A man named Elwood Haynes wanted to know about our bearings. He was making gasoline-powered road cars—automobiles. This inquiry came to us in 1899 and he had been making his gasoline-engine machines since 1894, never more than a few each year. In that time most people thought of horse-less carriages as something still to be classed with perpetual motion. Not only were they considered impractical toys at best, but a dangerous nuisance. On the streets and country roads all horse-drawn traffic was disturbed by the sight, smell and sounds of a vehicle moving by itself. So serious was the hostility of horse owners that an ingenious fellow named Uriah Smith, of Battle Creek, Michigan, contrived a ludicrous remedy. Fixed to the dashboard, like a hunter's trophy, were the harnessed head, neck and shoulders of a dummy horse of wood. Previously this decoy had served, I suppose, as the sign of some harnessmakers.

We were not as excited as we should have been by the Haynes inquiry, though we were vigorously hunting new fields in which to apply John Hyatt's invention. Hyatt had said we should find a market for antifriction bearings anywhere there was a turning wheel. Already we had done some experimenting to prove that our roller bearings on the axles of coal-mine cars cheapened operations. Although our most important business was with industries where line shafting was used in the mechanical transmission of power, we knew this field was going to disappear. Even then some of the newer machine tools were getting their power from electrical units built into the mechanism.

So it was not long before Pete Steenstrup made a trip to Kokomo to see Elwood Haynes; and he got an order. That was the beginning of our real adventures. It woke us up. If one automobile manufacturer wanted something better than ordinary greased wagon axles, why not sell all of them? But we knew we should have to track much of the business to hidden places, to obscure little shops scattered through the East and Middle West. Literally, automobiles then were adaptations of vehicles made in carriage, wagon and buggy factories. The rest of the machines were improvised of parts made in a variety of shops. The men who were doing this pioneer work were, in the main, rather simple people on the surface. For example, Elwood Haynes.

The Haynes-Apperson machines, Pete reported, were made in a dirty little factory about as primitive as our own place. Most of the work was being done on a dirt floor. Pete soon was on the best of terms with Haynes.

Once Pete coaxed Mr. Haynes to come to New York. Because he had not been to New York in many years, Mr. Haynes brought his wife. When he came to see us, Pete asked where they were staying. The old gentleman mentioned a *déclassé* Broadway hotel that had become notorious.

"Mr. Haynes! That place!"

"Stopped there when I was here before. What's wrong with it?"

The fine old gentleman saw none of the transparent evil there. Yet his was the vision which was among the very first to see that the people of the United States might have better transportation than could be provided with horses.

Shortly after the first sample order from Elwood Haynes, we got orders from other builders of self-propelled vehicles, but always for samples, each of a special size and, consequently, a nuisance at the factory.

On the first big order he got in Detroit, Pete recklessly called me on the long-distance telephone. I could scarcely hear him. This, it seems to me, was sometime in the summer of 1900. He was returning East and wanted me to meet him at the plant on Sunday; he had a trial order from the Olds Motor Works. They wanted 120 bearings, four for each rear axle in thirty automobiles. Pete was beside himself, and so was I.

PART II

Pioneering in a New Industry

W<small>HEN</small> Pete Steenstrup and I got together, I discovered what a fine opportunity we were getting. Pete had learned from Howard Coffin, the engineer who was designing the Oldsmobile for R. E. Olds, that they might build more than 1000 cars in the following year. That seemed fantastic. If our bearing stood up—well, that was why we talked, sketched and planned all that summer Sunday. If this test order gave satisfaction, we might have to increase the size of our plant. Our engineer, Charley Lockwood, began drawing at once, according to specifications brought by Pete. This was, as usual, a rush job. Those first automobile builders were nearly always in a race to produce cars and get them sold before their scanty capital gave out.

A wildfire of experimenting in machine shops and barns was becoming a boom almost like a gold rush. In 1896, when Ransom E. Olds turned away from steam and made his first gasoline car, probably there were no more than thirty self-propelled carriages in America. But three years later, when we got our first order from Elwood Haynes, at least eighty separate business projects for making horseless carriages were under way. Despite failures, the number was increasing. Almost any mechanic who looked hard enough could find a man with a bit of money who would become his partner just for the excitement of owning a half interest in a gasoline buggy. There must have been hundreds of distinct species of automobiles produced in any of those early years. Most of them were so bad they challenged the mechanical skills and inventive powers of any who observed their uncertain chugging or tried to make them run. Nevertheless, that Oldsmobile was a good car for its time. In the year after we sold the first trial order of bearings to the Olds Motor Works, a tester drove an Oldsmobile runabout from Detroit to New York. The man was on the road seven and a half days. He was Roy D. Chapin, who later became an important factor in the development of the automobile industry. His adventure advertised not only the Oldsmobile but our bearings.

A 1901 Oldsmobile.

"Find me there?" said Fred Fisher. "I'm wearing a derby hat. No, that's Henry Ford. The other one was me. I was a helper; he was building an experimental car."

Pioneering in a New Industry

Speed! That was the most important word of all to Ransom E. Olds. He was a pioneer in the field of quantity production. Could we deliver what he ordered? My job was to make sure we did. But to Henry M. Leland, the most important word was not speed; it was precision. As the blackface comedian, Moran, used to say to Mack, telling of the outcome of an unfortunate experiment, "We found that out."

Shortly before I encountered Henry M. Leland, general manager of Cadillac Motor Car Company, I bought a car. We needed one for experiments at the factory. Before we could promote a wider use of roller bearings in an automobile we had to develop our own engineering. So this car I bought was to be a kind of guinea pig.

I remember going to every exhibit in the automobile show of 1903. Cadillac? Oh, no! We did not like the looks of that one-lunger, in spite of its reputation. Oldsmobile? Well, we believed you couldn't make cross-country trips in just any Oldsmobile. The car we selected was a Conrad. Remember it? If you do, you're good, because I had to rack my brain before I could recall the name.

Even so, it was a beautiful job—in 1903. The Conrad Motor Carriage Company, of Buffalo, had a comparatively long record as manufacturers of self-propelled vehicles. Unhappily, they had backed, so to speak, the wrong horseless. They went in for steam. Steam automobiles were numerous in the show of 1903 and afterward. Yet shrewd men in the industry saw that gasoline cars were going to dominate. Probably the steam cars were as good as the gasoline cars of that day, for neither was dependable. But it was evident then that the explosive type of engine had certain potential advantages for automobile design. No one can foretell what the future may bring forth, but the gasoline engine of today wholly justifies the choice made by the industry. Mr. Conrad, in 1903, had seen the light of reason; he was bringing out a new line of gasoline cars.

Those Conrad cars were the most tempting-looking automobiles on the floor at the 1903 show. They had been handsomely finished by carriage painters in a tone almost maroon which was called "automobile red." There were no running boards, just carriage steps, but there were patent-leather mudguards, which some called fenders. The front one had a plow-share shape. The individual seats in front and the tonneau, with its entrance door in the back, were upholstered in red leather like a biscuit couch. It had artillery wheels, a chain drive and in place of the then customary tiller bar, it had something new, a steering wheel. Best of all, it had a balanced look that came from sound design. I made the trade with Mr. Conrad—our roller bearings in a suitable quantity for his car, the price of which was, list, $1250 f.o.b. Buffalo.

While he was trying to excite further admiration for the carriage painters' work, I was fumbling at the bonnet. When I got it off—like a sewing-machine cover—I was looking at an empty place. There was no engine!

"Hey," exclaimed Pete, at my shoulder. "What makes it run?"

"Well, you see, this car was shipped to the show without an engine."

"But, Mr. Conrad, I want to see the engine."

Mr. Conrad caressed the paint with tender strokes, as one might pat a horse. "We'll have a motor in the car when we ship it to you."

"But haven't you an engine in these other cars? That runabout?"

"The truth is, Mr. Sloan, we really haven't built the engine yet. But the design is right. Mechanical engineers and automobile experts of this country and Europe have pronounced it correct." He had more to say and I remained "sold." From my standpoint, the car had one advantage—it lacked Hyatt roller bearings. By redesigning the rear axle and other parts where our bearings could be used, I expected to develop rules governing their application. Then we could evolve an engineering technique and make a more intelligent contribution to the industry.

What that Conrad touring car had under its bonnet when it was delivered at the Hyatt factory was a two-cycle motor. That was the thing that taught me how to swear! For all my technical education, I could not make it run. Various machinists tried their hands. So did Charley Lockwood; even old Mr. Hyatt. But the thing could not be made to give more than an occasional bark, after which, each time, it died an instant death. I sent a telegram to Mr. Conrad, and next day his son appeared. Automobiles were "sporty" then, and "sports" owned them. There was a silk handkerchief on display in the breast pocket of the visitor's suit. He took this handkerchief and stuffed it into the carburetor. Then when he cranked it, the whole mechanism shook as the engine caught the explosion and ran. With pleasant wishes, young Mr. Conrad bowed to us and left to catch the next train. He was good enough to leave his silk handkerchief in the carburetor. I don't think I ever did get a real ride in that car. The most we could coax it to run was a few blocks. Eventually, the Conrad was sold to Pete Steenstrup and a Newark friend of his. I planned to get another car.

One day Pete assured me if I would come on a Sunday to the apartment house where he lived in Newark, he would take me out for a spin. But when I arrived, he was in a fury. That day he had been summoned to court for maintaining a nuisance in the back yard of the apartment. The belching, the smoking and other offenses of that two-cycle engine had aroused his neighbors. Pete sold his half interest for one dollar. Later, so Pete told me, his friend, out of patience, drove the car to the Newark meadows and blew it up with dynamite. Lots of cars deserved such a fate in the early 1900's, but this was not true of the early Cadillac.

I remember how this was brought home to me. The white beard of Henry M. Leland seemed to wag at me, he spoke with such long-faced emphasis. He was the general manager of Cadillac.

"Mr. Sloan, Cadillacs are made to run, not just to sell."

On his desk were some of our roller bearings, like culprits before a judge. We did not ship bearings to Cadillac; we shipped them to Weston-Mott, who were making 500 axles for Cadillac, an emergency trial order. Under Mr. Leland's brown hand with its broad thumb was a micrometer. He had measured the diameters of several specimen bearings. Then he had drawn lines and written down the variations from the agreed tolerances. I listened humbly as he went on talking.

"Your Mr. Steenstrup told me these bearings would be accurate, one like another, to within one thousandth of an inch. But look here!" I heard the click of his ridged fingernail as he tapped it against a guilty bearing. "There is nothing like that uniformity."

Precision-trained Henry Leland seemed to be out of patience with all bearing manufacturers. But he had some excuse to be short-tempered with us, as I discovered when he challenged me abruptly, "Mr. Sloan, do you know why your firm received this order?"

As I started to answer, he got up, strode over to a window, beckoning me to follow. He pointed into the factory yard, where a lot of axles were piled like cordwood.

"The bearings in those axles out there did not stand up under the Cadillac load. The balls and races broke and crumbled. We canceled the order, but the manufacturer has continued to ship them. Unless you can give me what I want, I'm going to put five hundred Weston-Mott axles out there beside those other rejects."

That was a terrible threat. We'd lose the business of the Weston-Mott Axle Company. They'd have to change the design of their axle to use another bearing, which might end forever the relationship between Weston-Mott and Hyatt Roller Bearings. To Mr. Leland I spoke as softly as I could. Pete had warned me what to expect.

Clearly, it was up to me. Pete had pleaded with me, when he called long distance, to come on to Detroit.

"Old Leland's on the warpath," he had said. "I'm no mechanic. I'm a salesman. We're not speaking the same language."

So, I had come out to the Cadillac factory. To Mr. Leland's angry complaints, I had answered that pressure had been put upon us by another customer to make fast deliveries. Nothing else had mattered.

But Mr. Leland interrupted, "You must grind your bearings. Even though you make thousands, the first and the last should be precisely alike." We discussed interchangeability of parts. A genuine conception of what mass production should mean really grew in me with that conversation.

I was an engineer and a manufacturer, and I considered myself conscientious. But after I had said good-by to Mr. Leland, I began to see things differently. I was determined to be as fanatical as he in obtaining precision in our work. An entirely different standard had been established for Hyatt Roller Bearings.

Incidentally, a few years later Mr. Leland's rigid

[*39*]

standards were given a dramatic test. Three Cadillac cars, taken from the dockside by Royal Automobile Club officials in London, were dismembered and jumbled into a pile of parts. Thereafter, Cadillac mechanics, with wrenches, screw drivers, hammers and pliers, swiftly assembled three Cadillacs, which were forthwith started on a track test—for 500 miles. All cars finished with a perfect score. Nothing, I think, ever did more to establish the reputation of American cars.

This may seem inconsequential, but truly it is of great importance, because the ability to produce large quantities of parts, each one just like the other or sufficiently alike, within a predetermined allowance of inaccuracy, is the foundation of mass production, as we understand that term today. This conception has been the basis of American predominance in such methods of production. It is definitely an American approach, and even today it is still limited in its application elsewhere as compared with that in American industry.

The company which Mr. Leland managed had been formed originally to produce a car of Henry Ford's invention. Mr. Ford had resigned as engineer because of interference with his work, and after a year or so of trouble, Mr. Leland was brought into the company, which then became the Cadillac Motor Car Company.

My recollection is that when I first sat and yarned with Henry Ford was before he was established as a manufacturer. It was at the automobile show. Quite early it had seemed good strategy for us to display our bearings there.

Our stall was up on the gallery of the old Madison Square Garden. The front of it was a counter before which streamed an endless procession of spectators. The rear of our stall was the gallery's railing. Standing there we could look down on the main-floor crowd, see each exhibit, discover what the people fancied and likewise observe what was going on in the driving ring. Cars were put through their paces just as if this were a show of horses. It helped sales to show the customers that a car would really run. Indeed, up on the Garden's roof there was a towering ramp, an inclined plane, placed there just so the Mobile Steamer might demonstrate that it could actually go uphill. But there in the Hyatt stall we had a piece of unsuspected good luck.

I heard Pete hail someone in the throng passing the counter. A tall, slender man stopped and, after shaking hands with Pete, lifted his derby hat to wipe his forehead. After tramping around the show, he was tired.

"Come in," insisted Pete. "Where could you find a better place to rest? Sit down at the railing and see the show from a box seat." Then he introduced me. The visitor's name was Henry Ford.

Pete and Mr. Ford were on friendly terms. Pete had first found him in a little room in a loft building downtown in Detroit. There he was developing a racing car. So we three sat and watched the cars go round in the show ring below and talked, for hours I guess. Mr. Ford was tilted back in a chair, his heels caught in the topmost rung, his knees at the level of his chin.

Much was to come out of our association with Mr. Ford; fabulous orders for roller bearings. But I did not suspect that I was talking with a man who was to take a foremost place among the industrial leaders of all times. No one has made a greater contribution to industrial progress. I have already stated that the primary conception of mass production is a system of interchangeable parts. But it is more than that. It is the technique of the factory system, involving the continuous flow of these interchangeable parts through the various steps of manufacture, finalized in a continuous system of assembly. Right there lies Mr. Ford's outstanding contribution to industrial progress.

Besides Mr. Ford, many of the visitors at the show were thinking of manufacturing some sort of horseless vehicle. We patiently listened to all their stories, because we were so anxious to get every chance we could to introduce our roller bearings. But even Pete and I looked upon these people more or less as adventurers; certainly we did not recognize them as potential pioneers in the development of an industry that was to advance the economic and social status of humanity more than any other. It began in a pioneering spirit of adventure. But far more than that has been required. Give full credit to the pioneers and their successors—the scientists, the technicians, the producers and the administrators who developed with the industry. Literally an army of others, through concentration on their individual problems while working in many unrelated industries, contributed to its development through the evolution of better materials, better processes and advancing technique. Industry never grows merely as a unit. In aviation this phenomenon of industry is being repeated. Many technical problems involved in the airplane have been solved by the evolution of the automobile.

In 1905 a considerable part of our bearings were shipped to Utica, New York, and one day I learned that one of our biggest customers was considering an important change. Pete Steenstrup, back from a selling trip, brought the news. The Weston-Mott Company, of Utica, was being tempted to move its axle plant out to Flint, a small town in Michigan. I was interested—disturbed, too.

A set of circumstances in the automobile industry had tied us to Weston-Mott just as Siamese twins share a single blood stream. When they got a big order for axles, they likewise engineered a big order for Hyatt roller bearings.

"Are you sure, Pete?"

"Sure? Why, I had dinner with the Motts last night in their Utica apartment. Mott's taking his wife to Flint to see how she will like it out there. They've been offered a free factory site in Flint, next to the Buick plant." Pete had other information: The men trying to effect this change were William C. Durant and his partner, J. Dallas Dort. They were carriage manufacturers who had refinanced Buick.

That was a trivial incident of itself, but I believe it marks the first step in the integration of the automobile industry. Thereafter, bit by bit, we were to see a constant evolution bringing the manufacture of the motorcar itself and the manufacture of its component parts into a closer corporate relationship. All were to cohere as if drawn together by some magnetic force.

Industry has its own equivalent of military intelligence, and that was particularly true of the automobile industry at that time. Bringing news of the changes in the industry was a vital part of Pete Steenstrup's job as head traveling man of Hyatt. We had to do our selling while design engineers were at their drawing boards. Often we had clinched a sale before a company was formed to manufacture some new car. What we did was to induce the designer to incorporate Hyatt roller bearings in his plans.

All the roller bearings used in the axles of Cadillacs, Oldsmobiles, Elmores, Blomstroms and certain other cars were shipped by us to Weston-Mott; likewise those we made for Buicks. Here was my worry: How would this move of Weston-Mott to Flint be regarded by their other customers who were rivals of Buick? Would they be disturbed when they discovered that their supplier of axles was moving hundreds of miles to put up a factory next door to the ambitious, aggressive Buick? Suppose this move became a merger?

I was sure of this much: If one of them—Cadillac, Olds or Elmore—should make other arrangements for axles, Hyatt might easily lose some of its roller-bearing business. When such problems could arise to frighten us, we were obliged to keep ourselves posted.

Well, in that situation there was one strong ray of comfort: Mott was our friend. Today, Charles S.

Mott is the owner of one of the largest individual blocks of General Motors stock, and since 1913 he has been one of its directors. But about the time I was starting in at Hyatt as a draftsman, this tall, blue-eyed young fellow, a mechanical engineer, had been working in overalls. He and his father had a small business, manufacturing soda-water machines. Charley Mott, between classes at Stevens Institute, installed the machines in drugstores and confectionery shops. These appliances were hard to sell, but the Motts were pretty ingenious about it. They would permit a store owner to pay installments amounting each month to no more than he had previously been paying for tanks of carbonated water.

Then the elder Mott died and Charley went to Utica to work for the Weston-Mott Company, in which his father had owned stock. The company, beginning to make wire wheels for automobiles, was a relic of the bicycle boom, which subsided so swiftly as to make many persons feel that the automobile business, too, would be just another short-lived fad. By 1900, Charley Mott was superintendent, and Weston-Mott was making all the wire wheels for the curved-dash Oldsmobiles.

Then Olds canceled an order. The designer, Howard Coffin, had switched them from wire wheels to artillery wheels. So young Mott went out on the road to see if he could get orders for artillery wheels. Previously, wire wheels had been standard on automobiles; artillery wheels were extra. Thereafter the reverse was to be true, until the coming of disk wheels years afterward. But Mott, in his travels, ran into a serious obstacle.

Automobile designers were shifting from a tubular-frame construction in which axles were a part of the frame, to an arrangement in which axles supported springs and springs supported a frame. "If you want our wheel business," Mott was told, "you'll have to sell us axles too. Can't you make axles?"

Mott had never made an axle, but he was completely confident. He accepted all the orders he could get, until the prospect began to look rather more tempting than the vanished wire-wheel business. When he went home to Utica to figure how the axles should be made, he had $250,000 worth of orders. One of the first was a trial order for 500 sets of axles for Cadillac.

Mott, to make his first axle, took a cold-drawn tube and turned it in a lathe until the inside was smooth. Then he fitted inside of this a cold-rolled shafting on which he placed four Hyatt roller bearings. Although they started with cold-rolled shafting, soon they got to using high-carbon shafting, after which there were many improvements; first a hardened sleeve in the tube, then a sleeve on the axle. The first bearings were not ground. I have previously told how Henry Leland showed me how and why we had to do our manufacturing on a precision basis. Anyway, Weston-Mott and Hyatt were interdependent to an extraordinary degree.

It was not long before Charley Mott had given me assurance that he was still the boss of his business, in spite of his move to Flint. Nevertheless, to finance the building of his new Flint plant, he had been compelled to sell an interest in Weston-Mott to the Buick people. As I recall it, the arrangement provided for the writing of $500,000 worth of stock. Mott and his partner, W. G. Doolittle, calculated that their assets were worth $400,000. Durant and Dort provided them with $100,000 cash, so that they would have sufficient capital to move and build a new plant. As far as capital shortage went, most of us were in similar situations then. Orders grew and grew, but so did our financial problems. You would use every dollar you could get to put into bearings to make more dollars to buy more machinery to make more and more bearings. Whether you made axles, engines, wheels, bodies, lamps or hardware, it was the same story. All of us were trying to capitalize the boom and having a hard time doing it.

Why had Durant and Dort been so anxious to get Weston-Mott's axle plant established next door to the

Mr. Sloan, Harry Carroll, advertising manager of Hyatt Roller Bearing Company, and Henry Ewald of Campbell, Ewald Company, in 1911. The latter firm had the Hyatt account.

Mr. and Mrs. Alfred P. Sloan, Sr.

new Buick factory in Flint? Every piece of the motor-car is essential in the sense that the automobile is not complete unless every part is available. Delay in delivery of any part stops the work. A dependable supply of parts might well make the difference between success and failure. Distance added uncertainty. It was natural, therefore, for the industry to correlate all its manufacturing within a rather narrow geographical area. It was a practical urge, but underneath it was a very definite economic justification.

There is not space here to unravel all the factors involving industry's evolution, but I have strong feelings against the practice of grouping factory after factory, when wholly unrelated to one another, in unhealthy masses. I believe we should move toward a better balance between industry and the land. There is no one so hopeless as a worker specialized in industry who finds himself without a job and with a family to care for, who is marooned in an industrial center today. It is my idea that industry should seek every sound opportunity to scatter its productivity around the country in strategic locations.

Weston-Mott continued some operations in its Utica plant after the new one was established in Flint, and we had to keep in touch with both, of course. I liked to work with Mott. His training had made him methodical. When he was confronted by a problem, he tackled it as I did my own, with engineering care to get the facts. Neither one of us ever took any pride in hunches. We left all the glory of that kind of thinking to such men as liked to be labeled "genius." We much preferred the slow process of getting all the available facts, analyzing them as completely as our experience and ability made possible, and then deciding our course. One of Mott's right-hand men was Harry Bassett. In later years he was the man Walter Chrysler chose to succeed him in command of Buick. He was a kind of axle-making wizard. Harry Bassett and Pete Steenstrup were fast friends.

Sometimes Pete's friendships, made on behalf of Hyatt Roller Bearings, were a trial to me. I remember once when Pete insisted that, for the sake of business, I must accompany him and one of our customers to Atlantic City. This trip was one I dreaded. I liked working with that customer, but playing with him was another matter. He played as he worked—hard. It was hot when we arrived at our Boardwalk hotel.

In horror I heard them schedule the program: We should visit all the cafés in Atlantic City. I needed rest, and it had been my idea to take a swim in the surf and then loaf on the sand. I whispered some of my feelings to Pete.

"Is that any way to sell, Alfred?" Pete was pretty stern about it.

"But, Pete, you know a couple of cocktails are just about my limit. What am I going to do all day and night? I just can't drink and drink and drink and——"

"Not even for Hyatt Roller Bearings?" There was mischief in Pete's eyes, but while we whispered, this production man, strong and thirsty, was declaiming that he proposed to turn Atlantic City inside out. Finding me stubborn, Pete compromised, "Alfred, how's this: Since I can't keep up with this fellow by myself, suppose you play around with him until midnight. I'll get some sleep; then you get to bed while I play around with him until he's tired, or something." And that's the way we did. Being a good fellow seemed to be a recognized part of selling in those days. Pete was no more of a rounder than I was, but nothing was too much when he was trying to win the favor of a customer.

I remember how he campaigned to complete a trade with Ben Briscoe, Jr. When Briscoe wished to borrow money, he dared to rap on J. P. Morgan's door. Along with the Dodge Brothers, he had pioneered as a supplier of parts for the first quantity-production Oldsmobiles. In 1906, or about that time, he was up in Tarrytown, New York, getting ready to produce the first 10,000 of some 2,000,000 Maxwells which were to roll upon the roads of the United States. Pete finally got an invitation for Sunday dinner with the Briscoes in Tarrytown. We two were on fire with anxiety as he set out. John Maxwell was already sold on Hyatt bearings and Weston-Mott axles, but Ben Briscoe, we understood, had some ideas of his own. However, it was all settled when Pete came back to Harrison on Monday morning. He had confirmed an order for 40,000 bearings, which we would ship to Weston-Mott to be built into axles.

"Think what I had to do!" he wailed. "I spent my Sunday playing pirates with Ben Briscoe's little boy, Price."

"But why?"

"Well, you know Ben is pretty hard to handle, unless you approach him right. That was the best approach I could make. They had other guests, and I figured if I made friends with little Price, that would help me a little bit with Ben. He is devoted to his wife and children."

Pete gave me details of his day. The Briscoe home fronted the Hudson River; at the rear, a hill rose steeply. At a spot masked by shrubbery, the young son of the Briscoes had dug himself a cave. It was furnished with soapbox chairs, candles stuck in bottles, a few old cutlasses, some knives and broken guns. Young Briscoe was a bloodthirsty pirate and, for the sake of Hyatt Roller Bearings, all one Sunday afternoon so was Peter Steenstrup.

Pioneering in a New Industry

For a reason peculiar to the automobile business in its early days, the selling end—the selling, that is, of materials and parts used in car assembly—became more and more important. Selling the cars was easy enough; the insistent problem was how to produce. In that time, before we had a used-car problem, people wanted the new cars so much that demand was the most obvious factor in the business. It was overwhelming. This was so widely understood that at least 1500 distinct species of automobiles came on the market. The experience of all those manufacturing adventures, the what to do and what not to do, had a great part in the growth of the industry we know today. In world history there is not recorded any effort of production to compare with the motor-car technique. The reason is simple. Humanity never had wanted any machine as much as it desired this one. That was the fundamental force with which we dealt, those of us who came into this field early. No one has expressed what I am trying to say better than my friend, William S. Knudsen. He explains it all by saying: "Everybody wants to go from A to B sitting down."

The bulk of the manufacturing enterprises which originally contributed to the stream of parts flowing into the assembled automobiles was well to the east of Detroit. Many of those manufacturers saw only temporary profit in the chances which came to them. Most of them did not even go to the expense of sending their own representatives to the places were automobiles were being put together. As a result, Detroit swarmed with men who called themselves manufacturers' agents. They worked on a commission basis, a single individual sometimes trying to represent many factories. Often the relationship was on no sounder basis than a casual conversation.

"I'd like to drum up some work in Detroit for your plant. You pay me a commission if I deliver."

"Go ahead. What have I got to lose?"

I saw nothing of the mining camps of the West and nothing of the booms that happened where oil was struck, but I did see Detroit.

PART III

Two Big Customers

THE Hyatt Roller Bearing Company was dependable. We had to be in order to survive in the automobile-parts business. Literally, it was a capital offense to hold up a production line. If any manufacturer engaged in supplying parts failed to make a delivery according to schedule and thus held up an assembly line such as that of Ford, everyone would know it, from Mr. Ford down to the workmen who were made idle. You would not dare go into the plant the next time you were in Detroit!

Too much, too many jobs depended on keeping the schedule of deliveries. Consequently there were years when the express companies collected millions of dollars on "rush" shipments of tonnage freight that were sent express by parts manufacturers in a desperate hurry, trying to keep faith with their commitments.

No excuse was any good if you failed to deliver. Often in the caboose of a freight train that carried a carload of Hyatt roller bearings you might find a Hyatt man who would cajole, bribe or fight, as the occasion demanded, to keep our bearings moving toward their destination. Eventually we kept two men in Buffalo, just to make absolutely sure no cars of Hyatt freight could go astray.

Right now I can feel some of the pride and satisfaction with which I once heard Fred Diehl say something to me in the Ford plant. He was the buyer responsible for the purchase of the tremendous supplies that went into the Ford production.

"Mr. Sloan, there are only two concerns we can rely on east of Buffalo and Pittsburgh. Hyatt is one of them."

That was fine for us. But Mr. Diehl's remarks were prompted by the failure of too many suppliers to grow with the unprecedented opportunities of the automobile industry.

He went on to say, "They fail to keep pace, fail to anticipate the inevitable growth of an industry that is changing the old way of living. They have not the vision."

The confidence of the Ford organization in our roller bearings and in our ability to deliver was a most important factor in making Hyatt what it ultimately turned out to be. As I look back, I can see clearly that it was no small influence in determining my own future. I valued the relationship. I was stimulated by the drive for progress. The constant injection of a new and better technique, involving both materials and methods, was an inspiration.

Yes, Hyatt Roller Bearing Company *was* keeping pace. Our profits were constantly being reinvested to provide more and better buildings, more and better machinery. Mass production demands huge quantities of interchangeable parts and a factory system involving their constant flow. But likewise it requires a constant flow of ideas from the top to the bottom and from the bottom to the top of the operating personnel. In this way organization insures progress.

Lately I had an interesting visit with many of my old associates in the Hyatt plant, which brought back almost forgotten memories of those early days. There was to be a dinner attended by men who had served long with Hyatt. First, in the afternoon, I went into the plant. Twenty-five years had passed. Thousands were at work there. I saw many men who had been there when I left. But not so as to machines and processes. These had been replaced, not only once but, in many instances, two or three times. Hand operations had been superseded by automatic operations.

Processing speeds had been increased. Machines formerly fed by hand were now fed automatically. Better materials and better processes were making better bearings at reduced costs.

On that afternoon, in April, 1940, there was far too much for me to see every phase of the present operation. The last vestige of the old Harrison dump was gone. In its place was an acreage of factory floors in an orderly growth of buildings. But my mind kept filling with memories. I remembered my first visit, before the Spanish-American War, a rainy day when the last snow was melting. What I had seen then was a big shack in a big, black mud puddle. I remembered Mr. Hyatt telling me how the Hyatt roller bearing was born. I used to visit with him in the little shop where he developed his ideas.

Mr. Hyatt had not intended to design a roller bearing with a wide application to machinery. When he started, his mind had been challenged by defects in a sugar-cane-grinding machine which he was then developing. This machine kept clogging, and he undertook to redesign it so there would be less friction in its operation. Mr. Searles, who was to be the first backer of the Hyatt roller bearing, was interested in the sugar-machinery problem because he was head of the American Sugar Refining Company. The first result of Mr. Hyatt's work was a cane-grinding machine considerably improved; then it became apparent that the flexible roller bearings which enabled it to work could be applied to other machines.

Bearings were just one of many things developed without thought of motorcars but which nevertheless became vital parts of the automobile. All sorts of craftsmen were drawn into the industry through the chance that they knew how to make something useful to those who were trying to build vehicles that would "run by themselves." Who, looking at any 1940 model, would think that once a tinsmith could become, overnight, important in the automobile industry? Ben Briscoe did.

Ben Briscoe, when just a boy, had clerked in a Detroit hardware store. In those days many hardware stores kept a tinsmith who mended pots and pans or made things to order out of sheet metal. When he was twenty, Briscoe started a sheet-metal shop of his own. At first he had three or four mechanics, with shears, soldering irons and charcoal braziers. This grew into the Briscoe Brothers' factory with 1200 men manufacturing coal-oil cans, washtubs, pails and garbage cans.

Then into his factory came two men, one of whom he had seen before, R. E. Olds. The other was John D. Maxwell, a former railroad-shop mechanic, who had made one of the first cars designed by Elwood Haynes. Mr. Olds was ready to start production on the curved-dash Oldsmobile, so this must have been about 1900. In Maxwell's hand was a bunch of brass tubes, which, at a glance, suggested a musical instrument. It was fashioned in two rows of five-eighths-inch brass tubing, soldered into a header.

"Just what does this thing do?"

Ben's question was answered by Maxwell, later to be his partner. "It cools the water that circulates around the head of a gasoline engine."

Soon afterward Ben was at the Olds factory trading with the purchasing agent.

"I want seven dollars and a half apiece to make these things," said Ben. He got an order for a minimum of 4000.

"We want a lot more stuff, Mr. Briscoe. We want scats; we want tanks; and we want fenders."

Ben left the factory with an order that amounted to something like $100,000. Thereafter, for more than ten years Briscoe was one of the important figures in the industry.

He and his brother owned Buick at one time. This is how that happened. Ben and Frank Briscoe had a galvanizing plant, in connection with their sheet-metal works. One of their customers was Buick & Sherwood Manufacturing Company, a Detroit firm making bathroom fixtures. Then Buick & Sherwood sold out, and Buick engaged in the manufacture of gasoline marine motors adapted for farm use.

The Briscoe brothers, after making a quantity of fuel tanks and other sheet-metal parts for Dave Buick, discovered they were going to have trouble collecting. As Briscoe tells it, Buick said: "Ben, I can't pay you. I've been making an automobile engine on the side. It has cost me more than I expected. It's got a new principle."

"Let me see it, Dave."

What Buick showed Briscoe, his creditor, was a valve-in-head engine. A Frenchman named Eugene Richard was associated with Buick as designer and inventor. What they were creating was the first of the millions of Buicks. But this fact was not revealed to anyone then.

Briscoe agreed to advance $1000. After paying out several other thousands the Briscoes, to protect themselves, assumed control of all of Buick's interests. But finally Ben Briscoe said to Dave: "I'm going away. I'll be in Europe about four months."

"What am I going to do, Ben?"

"I don't know, Dave. You'll have to blow up, I guess. I can't stand any more of this."

However, Briscoe told Buick he believed he could

find a customer to buy Buick Motor Car Company, and he did. It was the Flint Wagon Works.

After a great deal of trouble and the vital help of William C. Durant, a salesman who had become a successful carriage manufacturer, the Buick business began to transform Flint from a small town into a roaring city. Durant had raised $500,000 capital for Buick, half of it right there in Flint.

In those early days remarkable progress was accomplished by self-taught men. Ford was a mechanic. Maxwell was a mechanic. Walter Flanders was a mechanic. The Dodge brothers were mechanics. Chrysler, who came later, was a mechanic too. These were exceptional men. Probably if each had remained in his native village he would have been an exceptional man, even if his accomplishments had been limited. They were original, forceful, strong charactered, ambitious fellows. In those years the American mechanic was a restless wanderer. Once he had skimmed the cream of experience from a job, he moved on to another in another city. There was something in themselves which made them seek places where skill could grow and opportunity could be found. They were not merely searching for a living.

Now what about today's eager and ambitious young men, eager to qualify for the more important responsi-

Demonstration of "Hyatt Quiet" in 1917. Countrywide tour of automobiles rolling on Hyatt bearings.

Blueprints. Automobiles exist first on paper.

bilities? That is a question I am asked thousands of times every year. Many are discouraged because they believe opportunity is lacking. They see millions out of work and cannot get jobs themselves. They do not see how further accomplishment is possible. But there is no justification for this feeling. Things are different! Importantly different! Yet the world is in no sense finished in its building. Men have only started. The greatest opportunities lie ahead!

Lately I sat talking about this with an old associate and friend, Fred J. Fisher, eldest of the seven Fisher brothers. We were high up in Detroit's Fisher Building. His office is a chamber paneled to its ceiling with beautifully finished wood, an appropriate setting for Mr. Fisher. He started out in life as a woodworker.

As we talked he showed me, with pride, an enlargement of a group photograph. In it were pictured about three dozen factory "hands." It had been made, he said, about 1901 or 1902.

"Find me there?" he challenged.

I studied the faces of four rows of men in work clothes; overalls, aprons, dark shirts that "wouldn't show dirt." Most had been wearing caps or slouch hats. Fred Fisher helped me hunt by saying, "I'm wearing a derby hat."

"Is that one you?" I indicated a mustached figure.

"No," said Mr. Fisher. "That other one is me. The

one you're pointing at is Henry Ford. That was thirty-nine years ago. It was the factory of the Wilson Supply Company. I was a helper. Mr. Ford was working on an experimental car. He just came out and joined the party. He wasn't any different from the rest of us. Probably I had a lot more photographs like this, taken here and there around the country. But you get tired of having them around and throw them out. You never expect them to become interesting to anyone."

That reminded me that when the nearest part of Harrison to the Hyatt factory was the town dump, a photographer would appear, drape some bunting and then, as the workmen emerged for the noon hour, he would get them to pose. Later he would come back and sell copies for a quarter.

The Fisher boys learned to handle tools almost as soon as they could toddle. Their father had a little repair shop in Norwalk, Ohio, and did horseshoeing, carriage work or any other job in metal work or wood that was needed in a small town. The eldest and the youngest of the brothers were born twenty-four years apart. Consequently Fred had been away from home years before the birth of the younger boys. He had his apprenticeship behind him and was a first-class mechanic, a woodworker, when he was seventeen. To learn more he left home; he hit the road. Thereafter he had jobs in Bellefontaine, Ohio; Richmond, Indiana; Akron, Columbus and many other places. When he had learned the technique of a factory, he quit. In big cities he attended night schools. He took correspondence courses because he needed mathematics to supplement his other tools. He took jobs only where superior work was being done. If you should ask him about certain towns, he'll say, "Never worked there. They were only making trash." One after another the Fisher brothers became fine craftsmen, but all of them, I think, owe something to the Odyssey of Fred. This respect for quality—almost an obsession—was ingrained in the Fisher technique. It dominates the organization today. Bill Knudsen said to me not long ago, when we were talking about the cost of G. M. bodies, "We just do not know how to make a cheap body." We don't. Fred Fisher settled that.

Fred Fisher became chief designer of the Wilson Body Company, and in a few months was made general manager, with his brother, Charles T. Fisher, as his assistant. Charles was a blacksmith. After a few years, when Lawrence P. Fisher had joined them, these brothers started their own business, the Fisher Body Company. One by one, until there were seven, the other brothers came along, first as employees, then as partners. They formed a second company when they began to make closed bodies.

When young, the automobile industry was peopled by adventurous individuals who were relatively young themselves. Furthermore, it had a sport side which had its value because the motorcar had not yet established itself as a utility. It was looked upon by many as a passing fancy. It was still a toy of rich men; expensive, spectacular, uncertain, dramatic; and it drew, as sugar draws flies, a host of persons who had strong appetites for excitement. But they made their contribution and an essential one too.

Mix with them? I felt I had more important work to do at the Hyatt plant. But the mixing was important then precisely because there was so little stability in the haphazardly growing industry. When a sales problem concerned engineering, then I could help. It was interesting when some technical problem involved a meeting with another manufacturer. It was fun to find myself at some convention in the company of men whose training and experience made us kindred spirits. Our minds moved together as sympathetically as meshed gears. We'd talk shop until we could not stay awake. But what fascinated us were engineering problems, whereas Pete Steenstrup functioned as our head salesman without regard to technological evolution.

Two Big Customers

If someone monkeyed with the ignition on Pete's Autocar so that only two of its four cylinders would fire, Pete, being a perfect salesman, would never let on he suspected what was at the bottom of this trouble. If Pete was playing cards on a train on his way to automobile races at Daytona Beach or elsewhere and became aware, through the hubbub and chatter, that the person who was fastening his shirttail to the car seat was Henry Ford, he knew what to do. He would slyly enter into the joke, pretend some errand and get up so hastily as to ruin his shirt.

Among Pete's business friends were the two Dodge brothers. John and Horace Dodge, while they were making axles for Henry Ford, were becoming just as important to Hyatt Roller Bearing Company as Weston-Mott. I began to know what people meant when they said "diamonds in the rough" after I met the Dodge brothers. They were hard-muscled machinists who had become manufacturers with a fanatical concern that any work should be well done if it was to bear the name Dodge Brothers.

They were born in Michigan and grew up as two rough, hard-working kids in Port Huron, where their father had a small foundry. In their later years they enjoyed boasting, in congenial company, how they had made their first nickels, dimes and quarters mending doorbells and leaky faucets and doing other repair jobs for the neighbors. They seemed to have been born with an intuitive understanding of mechanical things. Eventually they got into the bicycle business in Canada and in the 90's opened a machine shop in Detroit.

It is a legend among their friends that they equipped their first machine shop through a deal with the receiver of the big bicycle company which owed them money for use of a ball-bearing "retainer," the invention of Horace.

"You owe us money and can't pay. Tell you what: Give us our pick of the machinery in the Windsor plant. It's just about rusting away. We'll take it across to Detroit and start a business."

These two, who were to become great automobile makers, acquired wealth as parts makers and partners of Henry Ford. They made his first engines, after their initiation into the field as makers of transmissions for the early Oldsmobiles. They made Ford axles, too. These, like Weston-Mott axles, turned on Hyatt roller bearings.

Well, that made us almost the same as partners of these two, and in the same way we realized ourselves to be in an informal partnership with Mr. Ford. Every time he sold a Ford car he sold a set of Dodge axles and a set of Hyatt bearings as well. The Dodges, by the way, had a minor interest in the Ford Motor Company in those days. It was stock which they had been permitted to pay for out of profits on Ford business and was assigned to them on condition that they tool their machine shop to make the first Ford engines. Consequently, as Ford grew, so did they, in due proportion.

The Dodge Brothers, like the Hyatt Roller Bearing Company, became a unit in a complex structure of independently owned manufacturing enterprises. The integral nature of our various enterprises was as obvious as the diversity of actual ownership. Out of our scattered factories were hauled the trainloads of parts which were being assembled into a variety of automobiles.

Smooth relations with the Dodge Brothers depended on smooth relations with the Ford Motor Company. Fortunately for us, Pete Steenstrup and Henry Ford were on good terms. Their acquaintanceship began long before the name of Ford became famed. I think the first contact resulted from Pete's follow-up on a letter of inquiry from someone associated with Mr. Ford; Mr. Ford was building a racing car and wanted to know something about our bearings, what a set would cost him. In those days such letters commonly came to us mottled with the stains of oil and graphite. The desks on which they were written were workshop benches.

Anyway Pete had found Mr. Ford and C. Harold

Wills, who was drafting for him—if my memory is right—designing a car in a room on the fourth floor, above a machine shop. They could be found there only in the evenings. Each had another job by day. The place had no heat. They would draw until their fingers got too cold to hold a pencil. Mr. Wills tells how they would put on boxing gloves and flail each other until they felt warm. That was how they finished the drawings of Mr. Ford's famous racing car, the 999, the one with which Barney Oldfield made a lot of records. Its straight rear axle had no differential, but it turned on Hyatt roller bearings. Mr. Ford's first engine was already eight or nine years old; its cylinder had been fashioned out of a piece of gas pipe.

Naturally, we had an indifferent product in our beginning at Hyatt. Our costs were necessarily high. But all that was true of other parts, true of the automobile itself. To start out for a ride was an adventure; to return with no parts missing, and all parts functioning, was a miracle. I remember gossiping one winter night before the log fire in the home of a friend in Flint with the then chief engineer of one of the large manufacturers. As we discussed our plans and ambitions for the future, he said to me: "Alfred, I would really like to know how many millions of dollars the public has spent to educate this head of mine."

Then the public seemed to be willing to pay a big

price for an indifferent piece of apparatus—and like it. They forgot its shortcomings because it provided a new thrill. Fortunately before people's patience wore out, the cars improved.

As the parts of the motorcar became better, we continued to improve the standards of our Hyatt roller bearings. Our steel was not originally heat treated. It was used as it came from the mill. Today even young boys know that if the temperature of steel is raised to what is called its critical point, and then cooled rapidly, its strength to resist shocks and carry loads is greatly increased. But we didn't know this until the necessity of carrying greater loads on smaller areas led to the technique of heat treatment.

In my early contacts with the Ford organization I met C. Harold Wills. Seemingly, no one had any title in the Ford organization, but Mr. Couzens and Mr. Wills both had important jobs. Mr. Ford had determined that he had to have better steel in order to make stronger cars, at the same time avoiding the tendency to make them heavier and heavier. As a result of Mr. Wills' efforts, the answer was found in vanadium steel. When Mr. Ford prepared to introduce this new material into his Model T, I did the same at Hyatt.

This man Wills had started in overalls as an apprentice in the shop of the Detroit Lubricating Company.

After four years he was a journeyman toolmaker. Thereafter he studied at night, taking correspondence courses in engineering, chemistry, metallurgy. Today many big steel companies pay license fees to him for the privilege of making steels according to formulae of his.

Although Harold Wills was the one I usually dealt with when I had business in the Ford Motor Company plant at Highland Park, I was never there without sensing the presence of Mr. Ford, without knowing that Mr. Ford was the initial force. Each successive visit revealed growth and efficiency. They were gaining volume.

Volume justifies machinery and methods otherwise impossible. Volume makes possible a better relationship between what we call variable and fixed expense, reducing costs and justifying lower selling prices. I had been so busy trying to make more and better Hyatt roller bearings that I had had little time to consider the economics of Hyatt's position. I remember there was a period of four consecutive years when I was at the Hyatt factory every day from 8:30 to 6:00, except Sundays and holidays. No five-day week. No extra holidays. No eight-hour day. But my first realization of the importance of price as affecting volume was taught to me by Henry Ford. He had the vision to see that lower prices would increase volume up to the point that would justify such lower prices through reduced costs. This great idea has dominated the automotive industry ever since Mr. Ford had the courage to put his belief into practical effect.

One day when I entered the Highland Park plant to discuss the Hyatt production of bearings for the future, Mr. Wills interrupted me to say, "Maybe I'd better talk first." Then he proceeded to tell me that Mr. Ford had determined to make a drastic reduction in the price of the Ford car. They were going to make only one chassis. It was the time of the famous decision: "The customer can have a car of any color he likes so long as it's black." Everything was being predicated upon the increased volume that Mr. Ford expected; this would justify the lowered price.

Hyatt was in a stronger position than most of Mr. Ford's suppliers. Our product was a patented article. We might have argued he could not easily dispense with us. Yet I knew we needed him more than he needed us.

I knew my cost system was sound. But Mr. Wills was telling me that a due proportion of lower costs of our bearings resulting from the increased volume of Ford cars ought to be reflected in reduced prices for bearings.

"Look," said Mr. Wills, "we'll be taking the equivalent of 65 per cent of your last year's production. Don't you want to figure again?"

"Come down to Harrison, Mr. Wills. I'll show you everything."

The result of going over our books together was that Mr. Wills pointed out some debatable items outside the question of volume.

"Mr. Sloan, the only way we figure in your sales overhead is for a two-cent stamp when you mail us a bill." He grinned because this was an exaggeration, but he had a point. "Are you advertising in order to sell us? Why should you charge us for any of the selling overhead on the remaining 35 per cent of your business?"

A week or ten days later, after days and nights of figuring and planning, I went back to Detroit. I think we were getting sixty or seventy cents for our bearings. When I walked in, I proposed a substantial reduction.

Mr. Wills rubbed his hands together and said, "That's a boy!"

Now I have forgotten just what specific changes in our factory procedure were adopted to justify the lower selling prices that I made on this bigger order for Ford. One thing we did not do was to reduce wages; that was done too often in such cases in those days. But I had learned that increased productivity would support higher wages.

Two Big Customers

Primarily the automobile industry in early days was ruled by its production men, by engineers and master craftsmen. The demand for cars was so great the insistent problem was production. Ford was growing as no industrial enterprise had ever grown before. Hyatt Roller Bearing Company was obliged to grow with Ford, or else give way to some other supplier who would keep pace. The whole trick of that growth was to keep improving the technique of manufacture and to keep lowering the price of the car to reach an even bigger market. However, an even more amazing thing was the discovery that as the price of the car was reduced, wages could be raised. I well remember the consternation that spread through the industry when Mr. Ford made the dramatic announcement of a five-dollar-a-day minimum wage for his workmen. Many thought cars could not be sold on that basis. Who would pay the price?

At that time industry's practice was to set wages low, the lower the better. Reduce when you could, increase when you must. The power of an economic wage rate to stimulate consumption had not been realized. The five-dollar rate made good, but only because the Ford worker was enabled to produce more. From 1909–10 to 1916–17 the price of Ford's Model T was lowered year by year as follows: $950, $780, $690, $600, $550, $490, $440, $360. The magical result of that was a volume which overwhelmingly justified the cost of the factory changes which preceded each cut in price. In those same years his production schedule grew as follows: 18,664; 34,528; 78,440; 168,220; 248,307; 308,213; 533,921; 785,432. After that, two years of war interrupted the amazing process. But this is a long way ahead of my story.

The kind of things Pete Steenstrup had been doing for Hyatt in the early 1900's did not appeal to me. Once in a while in the early years Pete would urge me to go to Detroit, just to mix, as he expressed it. There were always so many problems at our plant that I would argue my job was to build the bearings. But Pete was persistent.

"Hell, Alfred! I'm not a mechanical expert. I'm just a strong Norwegian with a frolicsome disposition. I need you on some of my trips. Those fellows want engineering authority for what I tell them. You are the only one to answer their questions. Loads. Performance. Durability. Design. Above all, deliveries. So, you come along."

If I still resisted, he'd argue: "Don't make work out of these trips. Enjoy yourself."

Pete enjoyed himself, and without seeming to need much sleep. I've never known a man with more vitality to share with people. He could have just as much fun with Henry Ford, who did not drink, as with the Dodge brothers, who did. To Pete, three o'clock in the morning was not one bit different from three o'clock in the afternoon.

We gave a big party every year for all our customers. As a gesture to antifriction bearings we called those gatherings "frictionless feasts." Year by year they became bigger. Some years Oscar at the Waldorf planned them for us. Once, I remember, the cocktails were pumped from a fifty-gallon receptacle made in the likeness of a service-station lubricating-oil drum. Always it would be one of the big parties of the automobile show. Everybody in the trade came. In those days the show was at the end of the year. Entertaining and selling to manufacturers seemed to be synonymous.

The automobile industry's very heart was the Pontchartrain Hotel, in Detroit. Starting there, Pete assured me, he could track down anyone connected with the automobile game. Or, if a man preferred, he could simply wait in the clublike atmosphere of the bar. In a day or two, or at most a week, his quarry was certain to appear.

Back of the Hotel Pontchartrain bar, up near the mahogany-and-gilded beams of its ceiling and roundly framed in marble, ornately carved, was a clock. When its black hands reached 11:30 on any weekday morn-

ing there would be a crowd gathering on the mosaic
floor of the barroom and pressed against the green
marble, behind which half a dozen bartenders would
be frenziedly at work.

Detroit was on Central Time, but all those from
the East—accessory manufacturers, agents, salesmen,
racing drivers, journalists, brokers, dealers and others
—behaved as if their watches were set to Eastern Time.
Most were merely visiting Detroit on the hunt for
business. The joke with which they explained their
habit of assembling for luncheon at 11:30 was that a
man could not adjust a thirst simply by turning his
watch back. Actually it was a demonstration of the
degree to which scattered fragments of the industry
were still seated in the East.

The Pontchartrain was where motorcar gossip was
heard first. New models customarily had debuts there.
As word spread that So-and-So's new Whizzer was
parked at the curbstone, the crowd would flock outside to appraise the new rival of all existing cars. Even
on ordinary days, when the crowd thinned out of the
dining room, the tablecloths would be covered with
sketches: crankshafts, chassis, details of motors,
wheels, and all sorts of mechanisms. Partnerships were
made and ended there. New projects were launched.
So legend says, that is where Bernard F. Everitt, Wal-

Industry progresses today through science. In the General Motors Research Laboratories a cathode ray oscillator is used to record electrical events such as occur in a spark plug or ignition system.

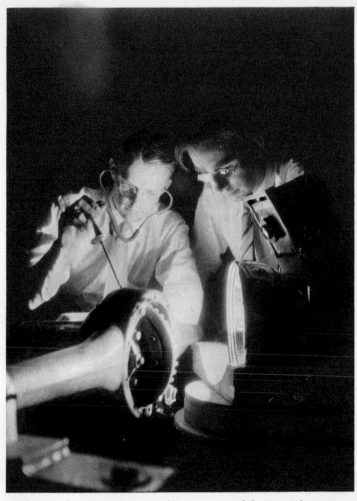

There's a lot of science expressed in your automobile. Research workers use a stethoscope to "listen in" on the complaints of a differential. The camera and synchronized stroboscope are used to take photographs of the tooth contact of the gears.

ter Flanders and William Metzger planned their E-M-F, which afterward became the Studebaker.

Pete Steenstrup and I were eating strawberry short-cake in Newark one day. We were arguing about something. The saturation point! People couldn't go on buying cars at this rate. That must have been in 1909.

Pete wanted to sell out and go to Oregon. Even though I believed another kind of selling was inevitable in the future of the automobile-parts business, I hated to think of any arrangement that did not include Pete. First, he was a close friend, and second, he had developed intimate contacts with myriads of people whose good will could contribute to the welfare of the Hyatt Roller Bearing Company. I tried to cajole him into staying. But it was useless.

"Pete, what is it they call Norwegians—all Scandinavians out in the Middle West?"

"Squareheads. Is that what you mean, Alfred?" He laughed.

His mind was set. He was going to raise apples. He felt some kind of loneliness, he said. He could cure it only by growing something. An apple orchard would be a good investment. Anyway, in a little while, he said, there might be so many automobiles the business would go to pot.

Pete's decision brought me face to face with the

sales problem. What was to be done? Well, I had no intention of meeting it by doing badly what Pete had done so well. I was convinced the engineering problems involved in the manufacture of automobiles would be the right approach to selling in the years ahead. I decided to organize Hyatt selling around a scientific appeal for the product. Consequently we needed an organization in Detroit that would render engineering service. I studied maps of Detroit and finally selected a site that seemed then far off, on which I put up a building to house Hyatt's Detroit headquarters. Curiously enough I bought the site from the young General Motors Company, which had taken it for a debt.

Nevertheless the Pontchartrain continued to be important. My appearances there were rare, but other Hyatt men were there. We simply had to have swift knowledge of changes in the industry so as to do our selling before the design of some new car was finished. For example, if John Maxwell quit Olds to join up with Ben Briscoe, that created a tense situation for all of us who were making parts. We had to know all the gossip. Our salesmen listened to everybody who might throw a gleam of light on the future, from Henry Ford to Walter Flanders' favorite bartender. They cultivated scores of sources: clerks, secretaries, newspapermen who were covering the industry, and obscure mechanics in key positions. Fundamental changes were occurring.

General Motors had been born. Closer integration was inevitable as the automobile industry passed out of the pioneering stage. But few had sufficient daring for the accomplishment of such vast trades as were even then in the making. William C. Durant was one. Ben Briscoe for a time was another.

Briscoe had solicited Durant's co-operation in arranging a consolidation of automobile companies backed by Eastern money. That fell through. Thereafter, Durant, adding Olds Motors Works to prosperous Buick, hatched out General Motors. Later Briscoe went ahead and organized United States Motors. Durant bought companies by the score, and for a while Briscoe was making similar deals.

Both of these men seemed to have an instinct for promotion and speculation. Neither was truly an automobile manufacturer as was Henry Ford or Walter Chrysler. But they both played other and important parts, especially Durant.

Every deal made by William C. Durant for another automobile company after he organized the General Motors Company touched the interests of many parts manufacturers. Repeatedly I was to discover that

Durant had taken over a Hyatt customer. R. E. Olds was making the Reo when Durant bought the Olds Motor Works, and John Maxwell, who had been its engineer, was associated with Ben Briscoe. None of us knew what was in store for the Oldsmobile, but Durant wasted no time in getting its plant started.

Mr. Durant sometimes tells friends how he drove over from Flint to the Oldsmobile plant in Lansing, riding in a Buick Model 10, a fine little car. No new Oldsmobile had been designed, so Durant got hold of the company's engineer, and showed him the car in which he had driven from Flint. Then he ordered its wooden body taken off and placed on a couple of sawhorses.

"Get a cross-cut saw," ordered Durant.

This was brought and Durant directed workmen to saw it in half lengthwise. Next the halves were sawed through at the middle. When the four pieces were placed together on the ground, Durant moved them until each piece stood inches apart from its fellow members.

"We'll make a car a little wider than this Buick," he said. "We'll have it a little longer; more leg room. Put your regular hood and radiator on it. It will look like an Olds and it will run. Paint it; upholster it—and there's your Oldsmobile for the coming year."

Buick's Model 10 was selling for $1000. The "new"

Oldsmobile was put on the market at $1250—and they couldn't build them fast enough for the trade.

Everybody said Durant was amazingly resourceful. Some said he was reckless to the point of danger. Perhaps both viewpoints were to an extent right, but neither really reflects the great contribution Durant made. Partly due to a too-rapid expansion, partly to an undeveloped organization and an inexperienced management, and partly due to the problems incident to an entirely new industry, General Motors became financially involved a year or two after it was started. A banking syndicate was organized; $15,000,000 of the company's notes were sold and a new start made. Mr. Durant retired as president and was succeeded by Thomas Neal, a Detroit businessman. In 1912 Charles W. Nash, a competent manufacturer who had taken an important part in the rebuilding of Buick, succeeded Mr. Neal. But Durant was not discouraged. Such men never are. He organized a new company— Chevrolet Motor Company, built around a car designed by Louis Chevrolet, a racing driver. He placed the shares of Chevrolet on the market, continually boosted the price, then offered General Motors stockholders an exchange of five shares of Chevrolet for one of General Motors. On the basis of the market price, the exchange meant a certain profit. After nearly four years of Mr. Nash's administration, during which substantial progress was made, Durant turned up at a stockholders' meeting of General Motors with stock and proxies giving him control again—an amazing piece of manipulation. He returned as president, and Mr. Nash established his own company in Wisconsin.

During those years the business of the Hyatt Roller Bearing Company had grown as never before. The plant is on the main line of the Pennsylvania Railroad. The people I met used to comment that every time they traveled past our plant, they saw a new building rising. We were pouring profits into new buildings, new machines. It was a time of terrific growth in the industry.

Speed! Do what you have been doing, but do it faster. Double your capacity. Quadruple it. Double it again. At times it seemed like madness. Yet people clamored for the cars. There were never enough automobiles to meet the demand. The pressure on production men was desperate.

However, I was not altogether happy about the increase in our business. The process of integration was raising a problem for me. Actually, we had two gigantic customers. One was Ford, and one was General Motors. Suppose one or the other or both decided to make their own bearings? The Hyatt Roller Bearing Company might find itself with a plant far bigger than it could use and nowhere to go for new business. I had put my whole life's energy into Hyatt. Everything I had earned was there in bricks, machinery and materials. I was, I feared, out on a limb. But I was not alone. Other parts makers were out there, too.

PART IV

Expanded Responsibilities

I HAD been worrying about the situation of Hyatt at the time I received William C. Durant's invitation to luncheon. One of our Detroit men had met Mr. Durant on a train traveling to New York and brought me his message first thing in the morning.

At once I was full of curiosity. Only a few months before, Durant had again won control of General Motors, after five years of being simply one of a minority group in the directorate. It was impossible for me to join him for luncheon, but over the telephone I arranged for a meeting in the afternoon. Then I took a little time to think.

The barnlike structure which had housed all there was of the Hyatt Roller Bearing Company in 1897, by this time, the spring of 1916, had gone. In its place there were modern fireproof buildings with a floor area of 750,000 square feet. Eighty per cent of that physical expansion had occurred in the three previous years. Our original power plant, a little ten-horse-power steam engine, had been replaced by a power-house that could develop 3000 horsepower. In addition, the heat-treating department operated its own gas plant of 3500 horse-power capacity. We had three private sidings from the main line to the Pennsylvania Railroad. We had our own fire department, a 300,000-gallon reservoir and adequate pumping facilities to protect us against fire. But there were more disturbing hazards from which it was less easy to be defended.

I was proud of our organization. We were as nearly scientific in our operations as a business could be—in that time. Our works were highly organized. About 95 per cent of the productive labor was on piecework, and I had installed an effective cost system. On the pay roll were chemists and metallurgists. Every step in the development of raw material into antifriction bearings was checked by scientific methods.

We had three sales divisions, each with its own engineering and sales staff. In Newark was the head-quarters of the one which promoted the use of our bearings in mine cars, in shafting; indeed, all classes of machinery.

In Chicago, a special division was handling tractor sales. Nearly every successful tractor company built into its product from five to twenty Hyatt roller bearings. But our mainstay was the automobile.

In Detroit in the building we had erected was the division which handled sales to makers of motorcars. We had contracts with Ford, Willys-Overland, Packard, Chalmers, F. B. Stearns, Hudson, Hupp, Chevrolet, Buick, Maxwell, Marmon, Mitchell, Paige-Detroit, Reo, and Saxon. We had contracts with manufacturers of axles, transmissions and electric starters. But one dismal fact was revealed by our accounting: More than half our business came from Ford, and our other big customer, General Motors, dwarfed the remainder. If either Ford or General Motors should start making their own bearings or use some other type of bearings, our company would be in a desperate situation.

After Ford and the General Motors enterprises, there was a big drop in size before we came to the customer next in importance. We were ready to step up our daily capacity from 35,000 or 40,000 bearings to 60,000. That would represent a gross capacity of $10,000,000 worth of bearings a year, a neat figure from which to estimate idle factory equipment, were we to lose one of those two biggest customers. We had 4000 employees and were preparing to take on more.

My fears were reasonable. The Dodge brothers had

started to make Dodge cars only a year or so before. In the trade we believed they had changed from parts manufacturers into automobile makers because they believed their biggest customers contemplated making parts previously bought from Dodge. The same uncertainties that troubled makers of parts were valid worries of those who bought our parts. Suppose Buick or Willys-Overland or Ford suddenly got the idea it might be cut off from an important source of supply? Lack of one tiny part might hold up their assembly line. That fear was the nightmare of the business.

Durant's luncheon invitation was like an alarming knock on the door in the middle of the night. It might be a sign I would have to make a decision about the future of the Hyatt Roller Bearing Company. The integration of General Motors was proceeding. What should I do? I saw no way to place the business under the wing of the giant Ford Motor Company. Could I wisely remain in the same status of apparent independence? Willys-Overland, third largest grouping in the field, then appeared unstable—at least many thought so. So there was small room for choice in the future. In my heart I felt I would be acting soundly for our business if I made a deal with Durant.

Original patents of the Hyatt type of roller bearing had expired by 1916. But I believed process patents and patents on our machinery fully protected the company for years to come. Nevertheless, only a fool would have relied on that in the face of such hazard. Already our biggest customers were insistent that in future contracts they be given the right to have our product made in other factories, should we fail to deliver adequate supplies.

At that time General Motors had offices in a building at Fifty-Seventh Street and Eleventh Avenue. I walked into Mr. Durant's office there about three o'clock; he didn't waste much time in idle conversation.

"Mr. Sloan, have you ever considered the sale of your company?"

"What's that, Mr. Durant?"

"Your plant over there at Harrison. Have you thought of selling it?"

"No, Mr. Durant."

"Are there many stockholders?"

"No. It's a kind of family affair. My father, myself. Also a few of his friends—Newark people."

"Well, would you consider sale of the property?"

"After all, Mr. Durant, it's a business enterprise. Why not? Provided, of course——"

Mr. Durant was smiling. "Mr. Sloan, if you thought of selling Hyatt Roller Bearing Company, about what price would you have in mind?"

Probably Mr. Durant really expected me to fix a price right then and there, because he was habitually buying big properties. But the Hyatt Roller Bearing Company was my life's work. I could not treat such an important transaction as if it were a horse trade. I told Mr. Durant I'd have to consult my board. He betrayed no impatience as I rose to go. His was the manner of a gentleman striving to be harmonious with the world. Besides, he had found out what he wished to know: Hyatt could be bought.

I arranged a meeting of our small board of directors. Besides my father and myself—together we owned 60 per cent of the stock—the board included two elderly lawyers, brothers, Edward and William Day. Edward Day was an outstanding lawyer of Newark. In his eyes, I am afraid, I still appeared to be a very young man to have so much responsibility. Nevertheless, from the beginning I had been allowed to run the business as I saw fit. I repeated my conversation with Mr. Durant.

My father asked, "Alfred, what are the assets worth?"

I pointed out that the value of the assets—the physical plant and equipment—was secondary. The profit potential, I insisted, was the important thing—the opportunity of the business to improve its earnings in the future. Actually at the time my father supplied

Alfred P. Sloan, Jr., and Charles F. Kettering examining the first electric, automobile self-starter, invented by Mr. Kettering.

Export business.

the first small installment of his investment nearly 20 years before, debts had probably exceeded assets. This stanch property had taken shape swiftly.

But when I told Edward Day what price I proposed to ask, he said I was crazy. Even so, my fellow directors authorized me to make the best deal I could. So I went back to see Mr. Durant.

"Well, Mr. Sloan," he said pleasantly, "have you got a price in mind now?"

"Yes, Mr. Durant. I think about fifteen million dollars."

Mr. Durant never batted an eye or ceased to smile, and his teeth were very white.

"I'm still interested, Mr. Sloan." Then he told me a little more about his plans; his great promoting talent was about to be exercised in arranging a combination of the most successful of the parts-manufacturing companies. He was acting for the Durant-Kaufman syndicate.

Two things had given me the courage to make this proposition to Mr. Durant. One was the fine shape of our business; this justified the price I was asking. But the other factor was my knowledge of Mr. Durant's way in such transactions. He was disposed to deal generously with the proprietors of any business he undertook to buy. He was not inclined to haggle over the price of something he really wanted.

Thereafter, Louis G. Kaufman, of the Chatham Phoenix National Bank and Trust Company, and John Thomas Smith were the ones I dealt with chiefly. Mr. Smith now is vice-president and general counsel of General Motors, an associate of mine. What they were forming was United Motors Corporation, destined to become an affiliate of General Motors.

Mr. Durant wanted to include in his combination Hyatt, the Dayton Engineering Laboratories, New Departure, Remy Electric and Jaxon Steel Products, which included the assets of Perlman Rim. Naturally, I had become well acquainted with the heads of these companies, especially DeWitt Page, of New Departure. As early as 1906, that company, previously making bicycle parts, had begun manufacturing a double-row, double-purpose ball bearing. Shareholders in these companies were being urged to approve the trade. The promoters wished the old stockholders to exchange their shares for stock in the new company, but stood ready to pay either in cash or stock.

I remember a conversation at that time with Edward A. Deeds, with whom Charles F. Kettering had started the Dayton Engineering Laboratories Company. I was impressed because his feelings were so like my own. Their position, too, had been hazardous, and for substantially the same reason. Their stake depended entirely on the goodwill of General Motors. What Colonel Deeds said was, "Now we can cash in. I'll be glad to get some real money out of this automobile game." For years, all of us had been obliged to put back profits as fast as they came in sight in order to expand with our customers.

We had seen our plants getting bigger with no possibility of protecting our positions by developing diversity of products or markets. Well, as days passed, Mr. Smith and Mr. Kaufman, on behalf of the syndicate, maintained that their idea of what should be paid for Hyatt was much less than $15,000,000. But I finally told them I would take $13,500,000, adding, "I'm finished. It's that, or nothing." And I meant it. I have always thought I could have got the $15,000,-000, if my nerve had held out—but it was a big transaction for me.

Mr. Durant then said it was settled, and I was told, "Mr. Sloan, you've sold the Hyatt Roller Bearing Company."

The transaction did not cause excitement in our family, because neither my father nor I discussed business affairs at home. I felt I had escaped a cause for worry, that everything I had earned since leaving college was no longer exposed to such complete risk. There was deeper satisfaction because my father had been put on Easy Street. He had worked hard. Yet year after year the tea-and-coffee business had lost ground. Finally he had merged with a wholesale grocery. This had not turned out well. I think he might have lost everything, had it not been for his courageous support of Hyatt. His comparatively small investment had brought him millions. Yet it was characteristic of him to keep silent at home about the wonderful return. He was determined that his younger children should not be spoiled by wealth. He scarcely changed his way of living. My father conservatively invested the bulk of his share, but I was led to invest much more than I had intended in this new company, United Motors.

They made me its president. At the time I had given Mr. Durant an option, I agreed to accept half the payment for myself in stock of the new company. But the others, father included, had been reluctant to take so much stock. They were not keen about the automobile business as an investment. Very few were in those days. There were to be 1,000,000 shares of United Motors, and in 1916 there was a wild sound to that alone. I think we were about the first ever to issue so many shares. Today the practice of having sufficient shares to keep units of ownership small is generally approved. There have been issued 43,500,-000 shares of General Motors common. However, I felt obliged to increase my holdings in United Motors to the extent that my associates in Hyatt declined. In consequence, I found myself with rather little cash and a devil of a lot of stock.

I have always thought that in the conception of United Motors Corporation, Mr. Durant had in the back of his mind the idea that sooner or later it should be part of General Motors. It was a logical arrangement. Mr. Durant was then working in association with E. I. du Pont de Nemours & Co. John J. Raskob had become chairman of the finance committee of General Motors Corporation. He was a man of brilliant mind. No idea was too big for him to grasp and no undertaking too great for him to attempt. He believed it was a wonderful opportunity to bring into General Motors these varied producers, so essential in the manufacture of the complete automobile. An important influence in his attitude undoubtedly was that these companies' organizations and personnel were needed in General Motors and would strengthen its management.

In the evolution of the automobile industry those companies manufacturing parts, generally speaking, grew out of enterprises engaged in business long before there were automobiles. Because of years of experience and successful operation, they had management, in many instances, superior to that of their big customers. Competition between parts producers had been exceedingly sharp. The purchasing agents of the manufacturing units were keen and aggressive. They exacted the last ounce of flesh. The result—urgent pressure for efficiency in parts manufacture. But with the automobile manufacturers the main problem was how to produce enough. It is not surprising, therefore, that as integration continued, the experience and ability of the former parts executives brought them to the top. So it happens that a great many important executives concerned today in the manufacture of motorcars are men who entered the industry through the parts route.

Soon after I became its president, United Motors Corporation's stock, issued to the public at 62, slumped off with other stock values. At the time the United States entered the war, United Motors went down to 10! That certainly put a big dent in my financial statement. But I had begun to see exciting possibilities developing for the future in our field. In accordance with Mr. Raskob's recommendation, in 1918 United Motors was consolidated with General Motors Corporation and later on was liquidated. I became a director of General Motors on November 7, 1918, and six weeks later, a vice-president. Stockholders of United Motors received shares of General Motors for their holdings. I do not know whether many would agree with my philosophy on the subject of investing one's savings, but it grows out of my own experience. I have seen General Motors go from eighty-five dollars a share to seven dollars, but never sold a single share. Speculation never had any attraction for me. Other than a few professional operators, who has really got ahead by stock-market trading?

Naturally, I like to see General Motors stock register a good price on the market, but that is just a matter of pride. Personally, I consider its price fluctuations inconsequential. What has counted with me is the true value of the property as a business, as an opportunity for the exercise of management talent. I have been most fortunate in being connected with a successful enterprise and I have gained by sticking to it through all the vicissitudes of changing conditions. When any man has formed an association in the early stages of a developing business—one that is producing something of benefit to the community or performing some useful service—his road to fortune, I believe, is clearly defined. He should help make it a success. Stick to it.

From the time I became president of United Motors, I saw a great deal of Mr. Durant. I was constantly amazed by his daring way of making decisions. My business experience had convinced me facts are precious things, to be eagerly sought and treated with respect. But Mr. Durant would proceed on a course of action guided solely, as far as I could tell, by some intuitive flash of brilliance. He never felt obliged to make an engineering hunt for facts. Yet at times he was astoundingly correct in his judgments.

One legend concerning him goes back to 1912, when a gathering of automobile manufacturers pooled guesses on the next year's production, each man dropping his slip of paper into a derby hat. That year 378,-000 cars had been made. Mr. Durant guessed that in the next year they would manufacture half a million cars.

The others gasped. They said, "People can't buy that many cars. Our industry will be ruined by such overproduction before it really gets started."

Mr. Durant mildly rebuked them, saying, "Gentlemen, you don't realize the purchasing power of the American people. I look forward to the time we'll make and sell one million cars a year."

Those men thought he was being fantastic. Actually, his vision was clear. In 1929 the industry was to make, and sell, 5,621,000 automobiles. However, this example of Mr. Durant's vision does not alter the fact that many costly errors would have been avoided had his practice been to base decisions on a comprehensive analysis of all facts and circumstances. He was invariably optimistic. It was easy to be optimistic, though, if you had been in a position to observe the booming growth of Detroit, Flint, and other places where cars were being made; and Durant had seen all of it.

Ford's announcement of a minimum wage of five dollars a day in 1914 had attracted men from all parts of the continent. Turnover in the Ford plant was cut down almost to the vanishing point. But at Flint, too, there was every desire to keep men, to stabilize the industry, to capitalize the boom. I remember that as far back as thirty years ago there were more jobs than men in Flint. Year after year, men arrived there in such numbers that latecomers would have to live in makeshift shelters. Rows of improvised dwellings like kennels were to be seen in vacant lots. Many lived in piano boxes. A covering of tar paper, a lid, a padlock, and one of these adventurers was sheltered. If he had a job in one of the booming plants, the workman was happy. Good wages with liberal hours to work meant big pay envelopes. No thirty-five or forty hours in those days; a man knew that the more hours he worked each week the sooner he could get a good home and bring his family on to Flint from wherever he had left them. These boom incidents were expressions of the fabulous demand of all people for better transportation, and the increasing rate of pay was an expression of constantly improving manufacturing methods. I myself did not think Mr. Durant was too optimistic about the future. But because of experience, temperament and education, I was not a Durant man. By this I mean no discredit to those who were.

Although I had become a vice-president of General Motors Corporation and had important responsibilities under Mr. Durant, our methods of approaching operating problems were entirely different. But I liked him even when I disagreed with him. Durant's integrity? Unblemished. Work? He was a prodigious worker. Devotion to General Motors? Why, it was his baby! He would have made any sacrifice for it, and he did make for it almost the ultimate sacrifice. But the question constantly in my mind was whether the potential industrial force under the General Motors emblem could be realized by the same boldness and daring that had been needed to enlist the units of that force. General Motors had become too big to be a one-man show. It was already far too complicated. The future required something more than an individual's genius. In any company I would be the first to say that William C. Durant was a genius. But General Motors justified the most competent executive group that could possibly be brought together.

Those who got on best with Mr. Durant were the ones who agreed with him, but I would argue to uphold my opinions. Mr. Durant was unfailingly kind, yet I am sure I was less than popular with those who prided themselves on being Durant men. It could hardly have been otherwise.

In bringing General Motors into existence, Mr. Durant had operated as a dictator. But such an institution could not grow into a successful organization under a dictatorship. Dictatorship is the most effective way of administration, provided the dictator knows the complete answers to all questions. But he never does and never will. That is why dictatorships eventually fail. If General Motors were to capitalize its wonderful opportunity, it would have to be guided by an organization of intellects. A great industrial organization requires the best of many minds. Yet Mr. Durant had no more sincere admirer than I.

The development of Frigidaire is just one example of his instinct for promotion. One day the Murray boys came to see him in Detroit. They urged Mr. Durant, as an old friend, to rescue their father from a venture which was causing him more worry and money than he could afford. The Murray Body Company was making stampings for us. The distracting enterprise was being operated as the Guardian Frigerator Company. As soon as Durant learned there was a factory in Detroit trying to produce and sell electric refrigerators in small units for household use, he was fascinated.

"Murray, next to the automobile, this is the greatest thing that could be put on the market." That was prophetic.

Durant went first with Mr. Murray to see what he had. This was a species of adventure often repeated in Billy Durant's life. He possessed rare ability to sense an opportunity in some inventor's attic. The Buick car had been scarcely more than an engine in an improvised body when it was first shown hopefully to him. In Boston, in 1908, a stranger said to Durant: "I can make spark plugs out of porcelain." He was Albert Champion, a daredevil Frenchman, racer of bicycles, motorcycles and automobiles. Durant went to his attic factory and made a quick decision to back Champion. He had him move to Flint to develop his spark plug. Buick bore the cost. The result was the AC Spark Plug Company, which has evolved into an important producer of parts and business for General Motors. So, when Durant accompanied the elder Murray up two flights of stairs into the disorder of a loft factory, he was having the excitement for which he seemed to live and for which he was temperamentally suited.

"How are you getting along?" He spoke to the inventor, a man named Van Russell from Milwaukee.

"Still experimenting, Mr. Durant."

"That costs money." To Murray, Mr. Durant said, "This man's got an idea. The rest is a lot of junk; a tin shop, some compressors and motors. You've got some refrigerators and are trying to insulate them well enough to make the idea practical. I'll tell you what I'll do. I'll organize a company with one hundred thousand dollars new capital, give you people a quarter interest."

Murray's associates accepted and Durant took possession. He moved the inventor and the junk, as Durant called it, to a little brick building at the Cadillac factory.

Then he said to the inventor, "Produce the best icebox you can make." To various others, as parts manufacturers, he said, "This is what I want. Can you supply it? We are going to do the experimental work. But if you can produce what we need, you can have the business."

He got the name through a prize contest. The minute he got hold of "Frigidaire" he knew that was right. It was so good it was almost a disadvantage; people came to use the word for any domestic-size electric refrigerator.

Mr. Durant had put his own funds into the development of the electric-refrigerator business before he sold it to General Motors. At a meeting of General Motors executives he shrewdly predicted this baby enterprise someday would be earning enough to pay all our salaries. You might think he had reckoned on making a big profit for himself. Not Durant. I'd bet my life he did not make a dollar for himself in that or any other similar deal. He was not that kind. I know that when he turned any enterprise over to the General Motors Corporation, the sum paid was probably a great deal less than he had paid into it out of his own pocket. In Frigidaire he gave the corporation the nucleus of a great industry. I don't think any of us realized what a magnificent thing he was doing. We did not then realize the great potentialities of Frigidaire. That was Mr. Durant's kind of altruism. Plenty of executives of corporations have acted otherwise, but W. C. Durant habitually behaved unselfishly. When he had raised that money with which Buick was launched into success, his attitude was pretty much the same. That was funny. Charley Nash, Dort and Durant each was taking a twenty-five-a-week salary. Durant had earned a fee of about $200,000 worth of Buick stock, but he turned this over to the Durant-Dort Carriage Company simply because he had promoted Buick "on company time."

When I say that in his approach to business administration Mr. Durant was like a dictator, I do not mean to suggest that he was ever ruthless; he was much too benevolent for that. But if Mr. Durant got an idea for a new model, whether it fitted into the General Motors scheme, or whether it suited the executive responsible for the subsidiary company whose name this car would bear, he felt free to proceed with its manufacture.

Now, he had sublime faith in certain cronies, and some used to say one of these men was unworthy of W. C.'s faith. This individual would receive Durant's ideas and depart for a plant in Michigan. Eventually he would return with a model, and Mr. Durant would send for all of us to come and see his new creation. Mr. Durant had a salesman's enthusiasm. A test of the new product was then in order, but, amazingly, he was content to allow the same man who had executed his sketchy directions and designed this model to test its performance. This was done by starting the car on a trip across the country. The story used to circulate that the "designer tester" never got very far. But telegrams bearing his name would continue to arrive from places farther and farther west. There were whispered hints that this man used to arrange for the dispatch of his telegrams by conniving with hotel porters along his scheduled route while he rested nearer home. That was one way of testing, back in those days.

Since 1924, General Motors has had the benefit of its 5,000-acre proving ground, a laboratory with a vast outdoor annex, at Milford, Michigan, where cars are being tested twenty-four hours a day. Those tests are impartial. We don't want enthusiasm from our testers; we want facts, and we provide scientific apparatus to insure scientific answers.

I was aghast in those days when Mr. Durant would display a telegram from his aide who was both designer and tester. He would say, "See this message? Oh, that's a wonderful car." Eventually, this master salesman's optimism, unchecked by facts, became downright disturbing to men who really loved him, men whose fortunes he had increased many fold. Should they blindly, mutely risk loss of those fortunes?

One cause of Mr. Durant's difficulties with subordinates was that he tried to carry everything in his head. When some thought flashed through his mind he was disposed to act on it forthwith, and rarely troubled to consult with the man who had the real responsibility. I remember advising him we ought to have an audit. I explained that I thought a business as big as General Motors should have its accounts examined by independent auditors. Stockholders had a right to an independent appraisal of what we were doing.

"Whom would you recommend?"

I named a firm that had served me at Hyatt and United Motors. I was on the operating side and had nothing to do with the financial end. Nevertheless, Mr. Durant immediately gave me instructions: "Go get them; make a deal, you are right." Thus, for the first time General Motors books were audited by certified public accountants. Yet even when this sort of interference struck as a lightning bolt into your own department, you did not protest, because he was so sweet natured, so well intentioned. It was just Billy Durant's way. You accepted it, and perhaps liked it because you liked him.

One time in New York I was invited into his office, and found him there with others discussing our need of a new office building in Detroit. One of the others was J. Amory Haskell, a vice-president, long associated with the du Ponts and lent by them to General Motors. They were disposed to purchase ground at Grand Circus Park, a downtown center of the city.

I had a point of view that I had reached after careful study in connection with the purchase of the office-building site for Hyatt years before.

Almost hesitantly, because it was not my responsibility, I volunteered an opinion, "Mr. Durant, I don't think General Motors needs to have its offices downtown in Detroit. We're not brokers. We're not bankers. Primarily, our purpose is to keep in touch with the various plants."

"Where would you put it?"

"Out on the boulevard. We can shorten the journeys of all who have to run back and forth to Flint and Pontiac. Cadillac would be close by. Much of our office personnel will be saved an hour or more a day. Why pay downtown prices for land? Or downtown taxes?"

"All right," he said. "Next time we go to Detroit we will go to the site you recommend and take a look."

We did so, and Durant told me to buy the land. His characteristic approach.

"What about price?"

"Whatever you need to pay. Just draw on the treasurer. I agree with you. That is the right location." We walked along the boulevard, and finally he indicated a place and said, "Buy up to there." How he picked "there" I'll never know; and before I had the purchases completed, I was instructed to buy the entire block. It was to become a $20,000,000 building enterprise, but that was Mr. Durant's way of operating; right out of his head. This simple incident resulted in the transition of this part of Detroit from a purely residential district to a business center second only to the downtown section. However, before the building was completed, General Motors got into financial difficulties for the second time, and we had to board up the unfinished building for a while.

That seems to me typical of Mr. Durant's method of operating the corporation. As it happened, the man to whom I assigned the actual work of buying the leases—Ralph Lane—did a splendid job. But notwithstanding a successful outcome, I contend that in a corporate organization of our size there should have been somewhere, as a carefully chosen part of the corporation's manifold intellect, some specialist giving all his thinking to problems in that category. I did the best I could, but it might not have been the best that was possible.

Mr. Durant liked having us around him. We used to go to the offices on Sunday morning, and while his barber, Jake, was shaving him, we lounged around the room. But always there was just one topic of conversation—business. That was no hardship. But it was disturbing to wait on Mr. Durant while our scheduled work was neglected.

Often when he called an executive meeting in Detroit, the ten or fifteen of us who gathered there would wait all day for the Chief. I would have traveled there from New York or elsewhere. Others would come from their posts in different towns. Walter Chrysler would have driven sixty-five miles from Flint. Often he arose before six to snatch a few precious minutes at his office desk. Sometimes he came without breakfast, because Mr. Durant always planned an early beginning. But whenever Mr. Durant appeared in Detroit, old friends could not easily be denied, and so we had to wait. One caller after another would delay him. There would be urgent telephone calls. We scarcely felt like doing anything else until he rang the bell, so tempers soured.

"Shall we go to lunch?"

"No, no! Mr. Durant regrets the delay. He'll return to you gentlemen in just a minute."

Sometimes it was four o'clock before we got started. Frequently, when he did get an earlier start, Mr. Durant kept the conference going without regard to appetites. Walter Chrysler used to chafe as he waited. Durant had fixed his pay at more than $600,000 when he persuaded him to stay in charge of Buick after Mr. Nash left in 1916; to be treated as if his time were of so little importance was more than irritating. He had terrific responsibilities at the Buick plant and as vice-president of General Motors. So did we all, but we had to wait until the Chief could get around to us. The poor man. He was full of problems of his own. However, the day came when Walter

[*116*]

Chrysler quit. Twice in our meetings the two had exchanged words with a flaring of tempers. Actually they were devoted friends, but on an empty stomach, and worried about his huge stake in General Motors, Walter Chrysler resigned.

There was never a minute after Chrysler's decision when we would have been less than happily grateful if he had changed his mind. We wanted him for his own sake; for his strength, his wisdom, his fine understanding of men.

Many events important in the corporation's history had been crowded into the months prior to Chrysler's resignation. In June, 1919, the stockholders had ratified an increase in authorized stock to $1,020,000,000. Thereafter, physical expansion was rapid. Negotiations were begun for the purchase of the International Arms & Fuse Co. plant at Bloomfield, New Jersey, for $1,175,000, and of the T. W. Warner Company, gear makers, of Muncie, Indiana, for $5,-000,000. The Pontiac Body Company was bought and added to Oakland. The Dayton Wright Airplane Company, representing assets of more than $1,200,-000, was bought. Biggest of all was the trade made for the corporation late in September, 1919, by John J. Raskob and Mr. Durant, with the Fisher brothers. They bought a three-fifths interest in the Fisher Body Corporation, paying ninety-two dollars a share for

300,000 shares of common stock. Eventually, this became a complete merger. There were other commitments that seemed far less appropriate. But earnings in 1919 had been $60,000,000. Optimism had seemed to be fully justified until along in September, 1920, when a change set in—almost overnight.

Everything I had in the world was in General Motors. But feeling as I did about the type of organization we had, I was worried. Incidentally, months after Chrysler got out, Durant negotiated with him for the purchase of his stock.

Durant, in his loyalty to the institution and his friends, always was trying to hold up and boost the price in the market, sacrificing his own interests characteristically in his efforts to do so. I felt he had about as much chance for success as if he had tried to stand at the top of Niagara Falls and stop it with his hat. Automobile prices had to go down. The world price structure resulting from the war had to be liquidated. It was being adjusted to a peace level. Everything had to become cheaper. But Mr. Durant insisted that we guarantee the prices of General Motors cars. He had come to the climax of his career, an optimist. He simply could not abandon something that was as strong in him as religious faith. Ford acted immediately and reduced his prices. All but General Motors reduced; they had to. Everything, if we kept on our course, added up just one way: ruin. I could not protect myself and sell my stock without being disloyal to Durant. That was impossible. I wanted to think this matter out.

"I'd like a month's leave of absence, Mr. Durant."

He was telephoning. Sometimes I used to feel as if he were always holding a telephone in his hand. I think there were twenty telephones in his private office, and a switchboard. He had private wires to brokers' offices across the continent. In the same minute he would buy in San Francisco, sell in Boston.

My fingers were drumming on his desk. It did not seem to me that the operating head of a corporation had any right to devote himself to the market, even if the stock of the corporation was involved. He looked up.

"What is it?" There was a fleeting smile. He was never too tired to be kind.

"I wish to go away. Not feeling well." This was no exaggeration.

"Certainly," he said. "That will be perfectly all right with me. Get some rest."

I went to Europe. In London I made up my mind. I'd return to New York and resign. Then I could protect myself, and with a clear conscience. So I bought a Rolls Royce car for future delivery. I supposed Mrs. Sloan and I would take a long time seeing

Europe. But on the day I got back and walked into the New York office I sensed something unusual.

"Where's W. C.?"

"Gone away. A month's vacation."

Queer indeed. He'd never done anything of the sort before. I decided to postpone my resignation. I was a manufacturer, and this could be made the grandest manufacturing enterprise the world had ever seen. I did not want to leave. So I said to myself, "I'll ride along awhile and see what happens."

PART V

Science, the Handmaiden of Industry

WILLIAM C. DURANT's difficulties were revealed suddenly. One day in November, 1920, General Motors was slaughtered in the market. The stock was being offered in increasing quantities. It was a part of the general liquidation that was then taking place. So many telephone calls for Mr. Durant were pouring into the switchboard that it was difficult to make a call from the office. Brokers were telephoning him incessantly. They wanted margin. Personal friends involved in the market decline were calling too. They wanted help and they knew he would always help when he could. No one was ever more loyal to his friends. But Mr. Durant's distracted aides could only say that he was away. It was Mr. Durant's custom then to go to his summer home at Deal, New Jersey, each Tuesday evening, carrying portfolios packed with work. He would return to town Thursday morning to remain until Friday night. On this day when the crisis came he had wandered off with a friend to get a little exercise on a golf course. When a messenger from the office finally reached him, the stock market was closed. But with all his skill and courage, with all the resources at his personal command, he was helpless. He could do no more.

But Durant, with an angry glitter in his usually gentle eyes, was at his desk the following morning. Some of the General Motors stock sold the day before had come, he suspected, from a member of a syndicate formed for the express purpose of supporting the market. I had no information about this. I have never had much need to inform myself about the ways of Wall Street. However, it was clear that a day of reckoning had arrived. Mr. Durant's brokers swarmed in. Their calls for margin totaled far more than he had. He needed a huge sum. I question whether even he knew just how much at first. It had all happened so suddenly. But there had to be an accounting now; stern, realistic. Durant and others held a meeting downtown in New York. It lasted all night. In the morning before the market opened, every brokerage house in the country that had a Durant account received from J. P. Morgan and Company a notice to submit a statement in order to be paid in full. The du Ponts had stepped into the crisis and arranged to assume Mr. Durant's personal obligations. To accomplish the purpose in view, they made an immediate advance in the tens of millions of dollars. There had been a vital need for someone to arrange a settlement with Mr. Durant's brokers for the broader welfare of the Corporation as well as to protect the investing public. Only the du Ponts had the financial strength and the courage to do this in such a critical situation.

In this way 2,500,000 shares of General Motors stock passed from the ownership of W. C. Durant to the du Ponts. In this episode W. C. Durant, a man of genius, of courage, of vision and great wealth, is seen sacrificing practically all he had in a fruitless effort to protect, according to his way of thinking, his creation, General Motors—loyal to the very end.

There was a meeting of the Board. Mr. Durant presided as usual. You knew he was grief-stricken, but no grief showed in his face. He was smiling pleasantly, as if it were a routine matter, when he told us he was resigning as president of General Motors. Our board meeting broke up. Later, as Mr. Durant left, followed by one or two devoted secretaries, there was only sadness and regret. A true friend had departed from among us. An epoch in General Motors history was concluded.

Mr. Durant was truly a pioneer. One of the happiest moments of my business life occurred a few months ago in Detroit, at the time of the completion of the 25,000,000th car produced by General Motors. To us, it was a momentous occasion. We had worked hard, with no limitations on time and effort. We had sacrificed everything to the cause of making General Motors what it had become and we felt we had every reason to be proud of our accomplishment. A big celebration had been arranged. We gave a dinner to the men and their wives who had served the Corporation for twenty-five years. There were over a thousand present. That, in itself, was interesting and impressive. Then we staged a pageant, showing the evolutionary development of General Motors. A sample of one of the very earliest automobiles was on exhibition, as well as one of today. And Mr. Kettering, in his inimitable way, told us about how the car of 1960 would look and act. Mr. Durant was present—having made a special trip from New York to attend the celebration. I asked him if he would be willing just once more to take part in a General Motors affair. He said he would, and gladly. So in due course I had the pleasure of presenting him to the audience. I explained that, after all, the 25,000,000th car just produced was like many hundreds of thousands of similar cars that would be produced this year. It was unimportant in itself. But in terms of accomplishment, in organization, in effort, it represented the accumulated work of thirty years. It was a symbol of an important achievement.

But too often we fail to recognize and pay tribute to the creative spirit so essential to start the enterprises that characterize American business and that have made our industrial system the envy of the world. It is that spirit that creates our jobs, so to speak. And, sad to relate, in recent years we have actually decried and attempted to crush that very spirit that means so much to us. Nevertheless, there has to be this pioneer, the individual who has the courage, the ambition to overcome the obstacles that always develop when one tries to do something worth while, especially when it is new and different. This is relatively true, be the enterprise big or little. Frequently we see how the smallest beginnings sometimes develop way beyond the horizon of the broadest imagination, as has General Motors. Thus I was able to thank Mr. Durant for the opportunity he had created for all of us in General Motors—now an army of 250,000—to accomplish something constructive and worth while for the nation's advancement and protection, as well as for our individual progress. I expressed to him the hope that since he had turned the organization over to us, he was satisfied that we had discharged that responsibility intelligently and aggressively—just as he himself would have wanted to have it done. The celebration of the 25,000,000th car by General Motors was an important occasion. But, to my mind, the most worth-while part of it was the opportunity that it made possible for a broad cross-section of our entire organization to pay tribute to W. C. Durant, who had the original conception of General Motors, and who was our first leader.

As I recall this episode, I begin to think about the situation that exists in business and industry in this great country of ours—a land of potential promise and opportunity—at least, so it always has been. As I write, we have millions of people unemployed, who seek an opportunity to work. Despite the fact that our government has been creating billions of dollars of indebtedness millions remain idle, and billions of additional indebtedness for national defense can have only a synthetic effect on the long range fundamentals of the problem. We have hundreds of millions of dollars lying idle in our banks. And all this has been going on for many years. As a country, we are blessed, without measure, with almost every essential natural resource. We have the finest producing plants supported by the most progressive manufacturing tech-

Men and machines stamp out rear fenders.

Stamping press for turret tops, Fisher Body Plant.

nique that ever existed anywhere. A continually advancing technology—thanks to the resourcefulness of our scientists, inventors and engineers—offers additional opportunities for the production of new and useful things, as well as enabling today's things to be produced at lower costs and hence sold at lower prices, so more may enjoy the fruits of our productivity. As a people, we are willing to work, if given a chance, for the things that we want to improve our economic position and add to the pleasures of living. Yet in a land of such abundance we live in a state of relative scarcity, for too many have much too little. Too many have not even a job. And the remarkable thing about this is that so many seem to think there is so much mystery about it all.

For instance, some political leaders have tried to convince us that our idle money is a result of a static economy. But why is it static? They argue that there is little opportunity for further expansion and small chance to invest our savings in new enterprise in the future, as we have so successfully done in the past. In their lack of understanding they maintain that our unemployment is the result of increasing technological efficiency. They do not seem to realize that this is the only true road to greater productivity and increased employment through lower costs and selling prices, thus bringing our products and services within the reach of an ever-expanding market. They even talk about the desirability of a tax to penalize efficiency, with the objective of reducing unemployment—incomprehensible to anyone familiar with the workings of our industrial system. Then they develop a scheme of taxation, supposedly for revenue but actually resulting in penalizing business and industrial development, and so confiscatory in character as to prejudice the whole profit motive. Then they preach the gospel that accomplishment is a crime—the greater the accomplishment, the greater the crime. They teach the concept of something for nothing. This, in one form or another, has influenced our national economic thinking for many years.

Sooner or later we must learn that only by more work, and still more work—always more efficiently used—can we capitalize our unlimited opportunities; can we give employment to the millions of unemployed; can we put to work the billions of idle money and make use of our resources of raw materials, either in the form of more things for more people or for defending ourselves against aggression. Sooner or later our people must determine whether they are to support, as a national management, a group which to perpetuate its political power determines its policies through an appeal to the emotions of the uninformed, or whether we are to have a leadership which has the courage to determine what should be done on the basis of the realities, guided only by intelligence and experience. Expressed otherwise, shall we continue the system of free enterprise, or shall we accept the only alternative—regimentation of industry by a political bureaucracy, and we have been drifting very rapidly in that general direction in recent years.

I think the first conference I ever sat in with Pierre S. du Pont involved a matter of great consequence to all of us. It was when, with several other operating men in the Corporation, I went to plead with him to become president of General Motors to succeed Mr. Durant. We all recognized his great ability, his courage, and the confidence that would be re-established in the Corporation and throughout its organization, as to the future, with him as our leader.

Mr. du Pont did not want to be president. He felt it was sufficient if he continued as chairman of the board. But we had desperate need of his active support in the emergency that existed. It took much persuasion before he would believe he was essential to the rehabilitation of the Corporation. But he was, and he made a tremendous contribution in our hour of need. Actually, when he took office, protesting that he knew nothing about the manufacture of motorcars, General Motors opportunity for accomplishment was re-established and on a more comprehensive plane than ever before.

In the old Hyatt days when Pete Steenstrup and I used to walk up the railroad track to Newark for luncheon, I remember well how we—the bookkeeper and the draftsman—used to discuss the problems of the business. It was natural that we should think that if we had the responsibility we could do a much better job. That is human. And probably it is desirable that it should be that way. So it was equally natural, as I observed the daily moving picture of General Motors operations, for my mind to challenge this thing or that thing; to wonder why it was done this way or that way. To consider whether it would not be better if it were done some other way, and to build castles in the air—how I might do it if the responsibility were mine. It was clear to me long before this time that there was a real opportunity for a great accomplishment. A big idea and a big possibility had been given birth. The immediate problem was to weld an unwieldy and incoherent mass into a correlated and co-ordinated whole, by elimination and addition, through an organization based upon the fundamental managerial policy of first determining the facts and then developing the essential plan by capitalizing the group judgment of the most intelligent personnel that could be brought together—always recognizing the importance of an open mind.

Up to the time Mr. Durant left I had not had any direct responsibility for the manufacture of automobiles. My activities had been confined to the accessory group of operations. But I now began to have a broader scope as a sort of principal assistant to the president. Mr. du Pont continued to feel that he was acting as president under duress. He loved his home in Wilmington and disliked the obligation to travel all over for General Motors. Nevertheless, he gave us his time and the benefit of his great ability without limit until he resigned as president in May 1923, when I succeeded him.

The prime responsibility of General Motors now became mine. I believe it is reasonable to say that no greater opportunity for accomplishment ever was given to any individual in industry than was given to me when I became president of General Motors. I fully realized that, and I fully appreciated it. And I always have been grateful for the confidence that made it possible. I determined right then and there that everything I had was to be given to the cause. No sacrifice of time, effort, or my own convenience was to be too great. There were to be no reservations and no alibis.

Nowadays we hear a good deal about regimentation and free enterprise. Sometimes I fear we do not always know just what we mean when we talk about such matters. In the two years that Mr. du Pont had been president, much time had to be consumed in meeting the daily administrative problems. Many critical situations were constantly arising. At the same time we had to give thought to a fundamental plan upon which we could build for General Motors the place to which it was entitled in the great industrial scheme of things. The prime consideration in that problem was a definite concept of management. The first step was to determine whether we would operate under a centralized or decentralized form of administration. Decentralization was analogous to free enterprise. Centralization, to regimentation. All, of course, within the area of General Motors. We decided for free enterprise. By that is meant that we would set up each of our various operations as an integral unit, complete as to itself. We would place in charge of each such unit an executive responsible, and solely responsible, for his complete activity. We realized that in an institution as big as General Motors was even then, to say nothing of what we hoped to make it, any plan that involved too great a concentration of problems upon a limited number of executives would limit initiative, would involve delay, would increase expense, and would reduce efficiency

and development. Further, it would mean an autoc-
racy, which is just as dangerous in a great industrial
organization as it is in a government; aside from the
question as to whether any limited number of executives could deal with so many diversified problems,
in so many places, promptly and effectively. Of the
many policy decisions we have made down through
the years, sometimes the answers have been right
and sometimes wrong, but that answer was right. We
have never deviated from it. I hope we never shall.
After forty years of experience in American industry,
I would say that my concept of the management
scheme of a great industrial organization, simply expressed, is to divide it into as many parts as consist-
ently can be done, place in charge of each part the
most capable executive that can be found, develop a
system of co-ordination so that each part may
strengthen and support each other part; thus not only
welding all parts together in the common interests of
a joint enterprise, but importantly developing ability
and initiative through the instrumentalities of responsibility and ambition—developing men and giving them an opportunity to exercise their talents,
both in their own interests as well as in that of the
business.

To formalize this scheme, I worked out what we
speak of in industry as an organization chart. It shows

how the business functions from the standpoint of the relationship of the different units, one to another, as well as the authority delegated to the executives, also in relation to one another. I grouped together those operations which had a common relationship, and I placed over each such group for co-ordinating purposes what I termed a Group Executive. These group executives were the only ones that reported to me. Then I developed a General Staff similar in name and purpose to what exists in the army. The general staff was on a functional basis: engineering, distribution, legal, financial affairs, and so on. Each of these functions was presided over by a vice-president, the purpose being twofold: first, to perform those functions that could be done more effectively by one activity in the interests of the whole; and second, to co-ordinate the functional activities of the different operating units as well as to promote their effectiveness. In the General Motors scheme, for instance, the vice-president in charge of sales is a co-ordinating executive. He has a staff at his command. His contribution is in developing better and more advanced policies of distribution technique through research and in other ways. He co-operates with the sales departments of the different operating units. But he has no direct authority over their operations; that exists exclusively in the chief executive of the operation itself.

Science, the Handmaiden of Industry

The General Motors scheme of administration is founded upon the principle of free enterprise.

Important as a comprehensive scheme of organization may be, the administration of the plan involves the human equation. That means men—aggressive men —of experience and ability. There were many such among us. Manifestly, in any organization men should move from the bottom up to the top. That develops loyalty, ambition and talent, because there is a chance for promotion. Never inject a man into the top if it can be avoided. In a big organization to have to do that, I think, is a reflection on management. Of course there are always exceptional cases. As the years have passed, developing, as they naturally have, emergencies at times, I have been gratified to find that we have, with very few exceptions, been able to find right within ourselves some individual capable of assuming a greater responsibility, and he has always been given the opportunity. In the evolution of General Motors, as far as I can now recall, there have been really no instances where we have had to build into the top. I wish I could tell the stories of the evolution of the many wonderful men who now comprise the General Motors organization. It would sound like a series of American success stories, but time does not permit.

One day my friend Mott brought a man to see me whom he was eager to have in General Motors. He proved to be a big fellow. And as soon as I saw him I remembered him.

"You are Knudsen, of course! I had some business with you at Ford's some time ago."

Bill Knudsen, like myself, had come up through the accessory branch of the industry. He had started at the very bottom with a manufacturing concern in Buffalo that was making steel stampings for Ford, just as I was making roller bearings. In due course of time, this concern became a part of Ford, and Bill, along with others, went with the business into the Ford organization. He was advanced rapidly. Shortly after the war he retired from the Ford organization to associate himself with a friend who was in the parts-making branch of the industry.

Mott recognized in Bill a man who could do things, and believed he had the making of a man who could do still bigger things.

I explained that we wished somebody to serve on our general staff, to help our operating units do a better job, that we had, at that time, no special job in mind. He nodded. That was satisfactory to him.

"How much shall we pay you, Mr. Knudsen?"

"Anything you like. I am not here to set a figure. I seek an opportunity."

"How much did Mr. Ford pay you?"

"Fifty thousand dollars."

Science, the Handmaiden of Industry

Shortly after Mr. Knudsen's entry into our organization, I transferred him to Chevrolet in complete charge of manufacture. It was not long after that he was made general manager and chief executive of the Chevrolet Motor Division, in complete charge of that entire business.

There is no need of repeating the story of how Chevrolet grew and grew, until it gained world leadership among the motorcars in the low-priced field, and how it has successfully maintained that leadership, as the years have passed, standing today at the very top of its long and successful career.

As I proudly make that observation there comes into my mind a rather interesting incident.

At the time Mr. du Pont became president, someone had the idea of having a survey made of the General Motors properties, with recommendations as to what might be done in the way of a reconstruction program. The job was entrusted to a firm of consulting engineers of high standing. The most illuminating recommendation was that the whole Chevrolet operation should be liquidated. There was no chance to make it a profitable business. We could not hope to compete. I was much upset because I feared the prestige of the authors might overcome our arguments to the contrary. So I went to Mr. du Pont and told him what we thought we might accomplish if we built

[*139*]

a good product and sold it aggressively. We urged upon him the fact that many more people always could buy low-priced cars than Cadillacs and even Buicks. That it was an insult to say we could not compete with anyone. It was a case of ability and hard work. He listened most patiently, and finally said, "Forget the report. We will go ahead and see what we can do." Mr. du Pont was always that way. He had the courage of his convictions. Facts were the only things that counted. So Chevrolet was saved and General Motors avoided what would have been a catastrophe.

The great difference in managerial technique between the industry of today as compared with that of yesterday is what might be referred to as the necessity of the scientific approach, the elimination of operation by hunches; this affects men, tools and methods. Many associate the word scientific with physics. But it means much more than that. Scientific management means a constant search for the facts, the true actualities, and their intelligent, unprejudiced analysis. Thus, and in no other way, policies and their administration are determined. I keep saying to the General Motors organization that we are prepared to spend any proper amount of money to get the facts. Only by increased knowledge can we progress, perhaps I had better say survive. That is really research, but few realize that research can and should be just as effectively used in all functional branches of industry as in physics. Research into the problem of distribution, for instance, has paid General Motors big dividends. Again it is the scientific approach. I keep mentioning it because it seems to me the willingness and ability to apply such methods might well determine the extent of success of any enterprise, and the larger the enterprise, the more vital it becomes. I had thought much about all this as an executive working under Mr. Durant; hence it was natural, as chief executive of the corporation, that I should turn to that type of managerial approach. The answer would be found in the facts.

In no industry could the product be more important than in the automotive industry, and every year it is different. Here is involved the engineering application of the scientific approach. I have already told the story of how the cars were sometimes tested. I realized that General Motors would be judged by its products. I would start right there at the beginning. I determined that my first job would be to concentrate all effort possible on making General Motors cars the very top in eye appeal, in engineering soundness, and in technological progress. Up to this time our engineers and their staffs had less than a secondary place in the scheme of organization. I determined that no money should be spared in equipment and personnel. I began to encourage better engineering by taking an active part in the work myself. I became chairman of a technical committee to which all our chief engineering executives belonged. Engineers appreciate scientific tools to work with. They had had in some cases really nothing. Now they had everything needed by them. We all worked together to make General Motors cars what they represent today.

The General Motors Proving Ground illustrates one step toward that objective. Here is the story: I was in Europe on business, and became interested in four-wheel brakes. I believed they would in time be an essential in motorcar design. This was before they were used to any extent anywhere. I sought out an engineer named Perrott; who had done much experimental work with four-wheel brakes in France, brought him back on the ship with me and sent him to Detroit so we would have available the best advice. All our engineering divisions were interested, and all but one wanted to go ahead. After the preliminary designs were laid out and samples produced, I arranged an engineering demonstration.

We went to a place back of Pontiac, Michigan, which was convenient to all, intending to run some tests. We had seven or eight cars, and quite a large party of executives and engineers. It was a public road, and as our tests had to be conducted at speed we would no sooner get started than it was necessary for us to stop because someone would come driving along the road. The futility of a great organization doing its engineering work under such conditions became overwhelmingly apparent to me as I waited time after time to get the tests started and then restarted.

That was hardly a scientific approach and it started in my mind the idea of a great outdoor laboratory, complete with all types of roads that existed anywhere, so that the test cars could be subjected to all conditions. One road would be laid out for continuous operation at 110 miles per hour. That was very high speed those days. We would have hills of different grades, all carefully calibrated. Everything that was available in scientific instrumentation would be provided. Each engineering staff would have a place of its own, and it would all be operated under the guidance of our technical committee; and there would be a staff house, with sleeping quarters and commissary, so we could stay as long as was necessary.

It was a constructive idea and in due course of time it all came into being, even in a bigger way than I had dreamed as I watched the brake tests on the pebbly road back of Pontiac that winter afternoon.

My responsibilities had expanded enormously. At Hyatt, big as it was, I had been obliged to consider the interests of only a few stockholders, a few customers and three or four thousand workers. But as president of General Motors, I realized our thinking affected the lives of hundreds of thousands directly and influenced the economic welfare of many important communities, in some of which we were almost the sole provider. In some way, visible or invisible, as we expanded, the economic welfare of millions was becoming linked with the welfare of General Motors. Previously, when industry was smaller, the absorbing problems of industrial management were largely limited to the fields of engineering, production and distribution. Out of its endeavors in these fields had come a continuous stream of new products, providing new comforts and making possible better ways of living. General Motors was becoming large through a process of evolution, but only because it was rendering a service to the community. As its volume of business expanded it became able to do more for workers, stockholders and customers.

Large volume requires the use of the most efficient tools of production, and as the productivity of the workers is increased higher wage rates can be supported. By the same token, costs of production are lowered, justifying lower selling prices to the advantage of the consumer. And here also the worker profits by more work resulting from increased con-

*Workers and executives watch General Motors' 25,000,000th car
roll off the assembly line at the Chevrolet Motor division plant,
Flint, Mich., January 11, 1940.*

William C. Durant, founder of General Motors, with Alfred P. Sloan, Jr., its present head, at the 25,000,000th car dinner, 1940.

sumption, the government profits from the payment of increased taxes, and the stockholders from more dividends.

Bigness is essential in many branches of business and industry if the community is to be served on the best economic basis, and without bigness in some ways it cannot be served at all. As time passes, the necessity of bigness from the economic standpoint is certain to increase still further. Large-scale operations can support costly research, can carry new developments through the initial stages where losses are inevitable. A dynamic economy is essential to progress and the continuation of free enterprise. It demands expansion and development. It raises our standard of living. A static economy means decay and ultimate regimentation. On the other hand, some see danger in bigness. They fear the concentration of economic power that it brings with it. That is in a degree true. It simply means, however, that industrial management must expand its horizon of responsibility. It must recognize that it can no longer confine its activities to the mere production of goods and services. It must consider the impact of its operations on the economy as a whole in relation to the social and economic welfare of the entire community. For years I have preached this philosophy. Those charged with great industrial responsibility must become industrial statesmen. Again we see the scientific approach is essential, because industrial progress becomes possible only as the whole community can support it by its own progress. It becomes a partnership relationship in a common cause.

An advancing standard of living means that more workers are becoming bigger and better consumers. Therefore industry's wage level is an important factor in this broader responsibility of industry because it involves the matter of purchasing power. It is one of our most important economic problems. Many believe the wage level is wholly at the discretion of management. That is not so if we are to aim for the greatest volume of production, the most employment. Because, other things being equal, as we raise wages we increase costs and selling prices. Economic law determines that. Higher prices mean reduction in consumption, less employment. It cannot be otherwise. I wish most sincerely that there could be a broader recognition of the fundamental economic fact that the wage level depends on the amount of the productivity of the workers. Entirely so. Also the productivity of the worker depends upon the tools that the employer gives him to work with. The more efficient the tools, the more the worker produces and the higher wages he will inevitably receive. In General Motors we pay as high or higher wages than the workers receive in any other large industry. That is because, due to our large-scale operations and general policy, we provide our workers with the most efficient production tools, based on the very latest technology. If we stopped that policy our wage level would have to fall, other things being equal. The trend of the industrial wage level over the last twenty-five years has been continually upward, more so in industries that are progressive in the use of better tools. If this increase in the hourly rate had not been so greatly offset by shorter hours of work, the standard of living of our workers would be far higher than it is today. If any problem demands the scientific approach, this one does. Attempts to improve the economic status of our people, especially those who have so little, through hour-wage laws, shorter hours, and all the other panaceas that have been imposed on the economy in recent years, are nothing but wishful thinking. They may help a few at the expense of the many. They may form the basis of good political propaganda because the people do not understand, but the only true answer to the great question of more things for more people everywhere is more work more efficiently performed. It is a great blot on our intelligence that we cannot deal with this matter on the basis of the realities.

We hear much nowadays about the importance of security. I mean security in an economic sense. I think it is now in the minds of many who years ago never thought of such a thing. It is both desirable and undesirable; desirable because every one of us should assume the most complete responsibility possible for our own future and the future of those dependent upon us against the uncertainties of life; undesirable because too great emphasis on security defeats the spirit of adventure, of risk, essential for the pioneer attitude. Would Mr. Durant ever have started General Motors if he had thought too much of security? Would the Wright brothers ever have flown their first aeroplane? Would many of our other great industrial activities ever have been known? Too much security is the road to a static economy. In a static economy there is no progress.

I have emphasized the importance of an economic wage rate. Moreover, I think industry should lend a helping hand to its workers and to all its groups. This help should take the form of plans that afford protection against the vicissitudes of life and for the days to come when age prevents work or prejudices the efficiency of working. Organized methods will accomplish far more than leaving the problem to the initiative of the individual. Group insurance, hospitalization, plans to equalize the irregularity of employment are illustrative of what I mean. The latter are of great importance.

Science, the Handmaiden of Industry

The worker must live on a yearly basis, yet his income is on an hourly basis. He accepts the hazards of poor times—the business cycle—and in many industries, of which the automotive is an outstanding example, he is subject to what we call the seasonal trend. People persist in buying four times as many motorcars in some months as in the others, just as they persist in buying straw hats in the summer. This means many more cars must be produced certain times of the year as against others. The impact of all this on the production line means a varying number of hours per week. Part of the difficulty can be solved by inventory, but only part. With the work week limited to forty hours, there is no chance in busy seasons to work long hours with big pay envelopes, as we used to do; therefore the average must be less than forty hours and that is bad for the yearly income. Some urge a yearly wage, but that means either the worker accepts less to cover the uncertainties, or the cost of goods and services is increased when no work is available and pay continues, and this again means higher prices. In almost any business under today's great irregularities of conditions and with all the uncertainties that exist, to accept such a contingent liability would be dangerous and the danger increases as the goods tend to become less standard. This applies particularly to the automotive industry where almost every car is built to specifications as to color, trim, and in other ways, and all unsold cars at the end of the model year are subject to great depreciation in value.

We have tackled this problem of the seasonal trend in the workman's interest. At the beginning of the year we guarantee every worker of five years' standing 60 per cent of his normal 40 hours' pay every week up to the limits of the plan. This helps him to budget his income against his expenses. In those weeks where we are unable to give him 24 hours' work, on the worker's request we advance the difference in his pay envelope, up to a total of 360 hours' work. He pays it back to us when he has work in excess of 24 hours, to the extent of one half of this excess, and without interest. If he leaves or dies the advance is canceled. Such a plan helps to equalize the seasonal difficulty, but of course does not protect the worker against the long swings of our business ups and downs any more than the stockholders or suppliers or others are protected. When the national income shrinks all must take less—there is no way out.

In 1919 General Motors inaugurated an employes' savings and investment plan. Any employe was permitted to pay into the Savings Fund 10 per cent of his earnings, up to $300 a year. For each dollar of savings paid in, the corporation made a contribution designed to stimulate thrift and help the employe to provide for his future. Interest was guaranteed on the employe's payments while the corporation invested its contribution and the income thereon in its common stock. Each year a new "series" began, after the fashion of building and loan savings organizations. These "paid out" at the end of five years. But if any employe chose to make payments on a home he was entitled to receive the same share in the corporation's contribution as if his savings had been left on deposit with the company. A total of 43,000 have thus become home owners.

The first series of 1919 matured at the end of 1924. So, in January 1925, a large proportion of the employes began to enjoy the benefits of their thrift. For each $300 paid in in 1919 an employe received $1,007. This was a wonderful lift to the income. But in the next January, in 1926, when the second series paid out, an employe who had saved as much as $300 in 1920 received $2,714. In addition to this very real step toward social security for the future, every employe who had saved the maximum allowable under the plan enjoyed the comfort of knowing that through this organized plan he had on deposit with the corporation a total of $1,500 of his own money, which was steadily increasing at a rate far in excess of any other savings plan in which he might participate. Never in any year were the employes to get back at the end of five years less than two for one for the dollars they paid into the fund. From 1927 to 1931, for each $300 the amounts paid back were $2,241, $1,277, $2,680, $1,447, $1,054.

The varying amounts reflected the changing value of the amount of the corporation's part which was invested in its common stock. Of course such a large return was only possible because in this period, due to the rapid expansion of the business, the stock was rapidly increasing in value. In 1930, at the time of the great depression, General Motors employes had credits in excess of $75,000,000 which they could withdraw on demand to help them over the emergency. During the depression as the various yearly classes paid out there was a strong desire to keep the money in the corporation's treasury because the employes had confidence that it would always be there when they needed it. I always thought that was a wonderful expression of faith in our management. Unfortunately the Savings and Investment Plan had to be discontinued a few years ago, due to new laws involving legal technicalities, and in part because of the Social Security Act, which places on the corporation such a great burden of added taxes that it felt it could not do both.

But this was by no means all that employment with General Motors offered to all groups of its workers.

Think of the corporation as a pyramid of opportunities from the bottom toward the top with thousands of chances for advancement. Only capacity limited any worker's chance to grow, to develop his ability to make a greater contribution to the whole and to improve his own position as well. The routes to the heights in the automotive industry were open to all, even though increasingly and inexorably the big chances beckoned to those with unusual qualifications and with trained minds. The Fisher brothers had climbed. Chrysler had climbed. Knudsen had climbed. And in the General Motors organization thousands of others had climbed to some degree of eminence within the structure.

Can anyone see anything undesirable or anything contrary to the public interests in a process that permits and encourages the capitalization of the natural ability and industry of the unusual individual? Should we not honor accomplishment of that type? Should we not encourage it to the utmost? Do we not need that very influence in the grave problems that confront the nation today? Because the unusual individual raises his head above the majority, should he be held up to public scorn? Should we reduce everyone to the level of the mediocre?

I believe strongly that those managing our great industrial enterprises should have a real stake in the business. I believe it is essential that corporate executives be placed as far as possible in the same position as the joint owners of a private business. The amount of capital required in our great industrial operations precludes private ownership, but plans can be evolved by which the principles can be established and a more definite responsibility to the enterprise fixed. I believe confidence in management on the part of stockholders is increased when they see that the management has enough faith in itself and in the business to be a joint owner with them. At the end of 1939 the operating staff of General Motors had a stake in the business of $156,753,000 as measured by the then value of the stock it owned. We have consistently encouraged that idea, and, I am convinced, with profit to the stockholders and with equity to those who have developed General Motors to the point where it is generally recognized as one of the most important industrial institutions in the world today.

Primarily that line of reasoning was what caused the General Motors Bonus Plan to be established in 1918. Today this provides that there may be set aside as a bonus fund 10 per cent of each year's net earnings, after deducting 7 per cent on the net capital employed during the year. In 1939 this meant that before there was a bonus fund available there had to be earned for the stockholders approximately $80,-

000,000, equivalent to $1.62 per share on the common stock outstanding. Approximately 9,500 salaried employes benefited by the distribution of that fund for 1939. None received more than a 2 per cent participation in the total bonus fund. The important thing is that the bonus is payable in stock of the corporation, and as each year passes our executives have the privilege of becoming increasingly larger stockholders in the business—success or failure of which depends upon them, and them always, so far as the influence of management is concerned.

I wish space permitted me to tell about the many able men who comprise the General Motors organization. After all, what any one individual can accomplish is not great, but through the power of organization the effect of a few may be multiplied almost indefinitely, especially if the few have the capacity for real leadership. When General Motors took over United Motors, of which I was then president, they obtained several important units in the automotive parts industry, businesses which had made a name and which had developed real earning power as the result of capable management. Together they represented a tangible investment of tens of millions of dollars. That was all important in a way, but from another standpoint quite insignificant. It made possible the association in the

General Motors operating group of Charles F. Kettering. That was truly important. It must be mentioned in any story of General Motors.

Charles F. Kettering came out of the hills of Ohio. His parents had settled in a farming community. He tells the story of how in his early life he could have only one pair of shoes a year, and if they wore out in the winter he would have to go without during the rest of the year. Out of that environment, under these circumstances, came one of the technical geniuses of our times—a man who has distinguished himself as a scientist, an engineer and a philosopher. His accomplishments extend far beyond the horizon of General Motors activities, yet General Motors is greater because of him and his outstanding contribution to its technical development. He has been a constant inspiration for progress, a constant demonstration of the fact that the world is in no sense finished in its building. Every General Motors man bows to the genius of Charles F. Kettering.

The story of General Motors research under Mr. Kettering by itself is a romance. The development of Duco, with which all our cars now are finished, is an illustration. An almost prohibitive cost would prevent the production of today's volume of automobiles if the industry was still limited by its original paint and varnish drying problems. From the very beginning, in putting paint and varnish on cars, a full month was wasted by drying intervals before they could be rolled off the assembly line. Such vast storage space and waste of capital in inventory and delay in filling orders were a challenge to management. Kettering, searching for an answer, one day picked up a lacquered pin tray in a store. He found the manufacturer of the lacquer, told him he was trying to find a better paint for automobiles.

"Oh, you can't paint automobiles with this stuff. It dries too fast."

"Hell," said Ket, "the trouble with our paint is that it won't dry fast enough." He carried off a quantity of the lacquer. Somewhere between a paint that dried too slowly and a lacquer that dried too fast was the answer to the problem. Kettering and his staff, working in co-operation with the du Pont organization, hunted it down through scientific research. The result was the quick-drying, durable and mirror-like finish that was named Duco. Literally, it revolutionized the finishing of automobiles. The cost of the finishing operation was reduced, but even more important to the users of automobiles was the elimination of the repaint problem from their maintenance cost. A finish was available that would withstand the onslaught of all kinds of weather and maintain the luster of the car when new.

Without end came problems like these which had to be answered by our research organization in the name of progress. Who that rides today at sixty miles an hour, smoothly, cheaply, surely, knows that before we could have high-compression engines in our automobiles we had to have fuel that makes high compression feasible? We had to solve a fuel problem. General Motors part in the solution of this problem goes back to the time when Kettering was trying to persuade automobile manufacturers to replace the magneto with his Delco battery ignition system. The magneto produced just enough electricity to make sparks to fire the gas in the engine cylinders. You started the electric current when you cranked the car, just as in the first telephone you turned a crank handle to make the bell ring. A battery system which stored up electricity generated by the operation of the engine was an obvious improvement, but various automobile makers refused to adopt it, because they said it made their engines knock. Kettering knew his ignition system could not be at fault, but why did an engine knock?

Kettering and his staff determined to discover the cause of engine knock. One day they got the idea it would be easier to advance their experiment if they could see what happened inside a cylinder as the charge exploded. So they built an engine with a quartz window in it. But they could not see enough. Then somebody got the idea that if the flame was artificially colored they might discover more. They needed some dye stuff. The only thing available was a bottle of iodine in the first-aid cabinet. They poured this into the gasoline, and when the stained fuel began to explode in the engine cylinder a marvelous thing happened. The knock stopped!

This led to a solution that revolutionized the relation of the fuel to the engine.

But iodine was not adaptable as an anti-knock element in engine fuel because it corrodes metals. Here was a principle, but as yet without commercial possibilities. How could it be made useful? They tried various materials in the same group of elements—chlorine, bromine and fluorine. They tried them separately and as compounds. But none worked so well as iodine. From that they went through tedious, painstaking, chemical experiments to tellurium. Years elapsed, and much money was spent before they discovered tetra-ethyl lead. Small doses of tetra-ethyl lead mixed with gasoline reduces knock simply because such fuel explodes more slowly than ordinary gasoline. But how was this fuel to be made available to the whole industry, to all users of automobiles?

General Motors entered into an arrangement with the Standard Oil Company of New Jersey, because they had an important position in the refining and marketing of fuels all over the world. Each of us supplied half the capital of the Ethyl Gasoline Corporation. Only when this new fuel was available was it practical to design and market a more efficient engine, for by increasing the compression ratio a given amount of fuel would produce more power, or a smaller engine would produce the same power with a saving of fuel.

Today, 90 per cent of all gasoline consumed in the United States contains tetra-ethyl lead as a means of raising its anti-knock qualities and maintaining definite standards of anti-knock quality. Today the use of tetra-ethyl lead is essential in the modern aviation engine. It is safe to say no aeroplane leaves the ground without owing much to Mr. Kettering and his staff.

Due to the scientific approach fuels are now streamlined to fit the engine. A smoother, more efficient, smaller, and therefore lighter, engine, or much more power with the same size engine, means added economy to the consumer, and the end is not yet in sight. We strive aggressively to meet every engineering challenge by better engineering, supported when necessary by research.

In the early days, after operating your car during the winter too frequently you would find in the spring that you had to have your engine taken down for overhauling. Wrist pins, timing chains and other internal parts of the engine would be found to be worn and corroded. During the life of his car an automobile owner would pay a repair man for new timing chains. Sometimes a timing chain lasted only a few hundred miles. In places this trouble was greatly intensified. Research went to work on this problem. We found sulphur was the culprit. Many crude oils contain sulphur. When gasoline is burned in an engine cylinder the sulphur turns to sulphur dioxide gas. The hydrogen released by combustion combines with oxygen to form water. Water and sulphur dioxide make sulphuric acid. As vapor, this got into the crank case and mixed with the lubricating oil, which carried it all through the engine.

A simple change in design changed the whole picture. We put some windows in the crank case so as to introduce fresh air. Further changes in engine design were made so as to deal with the chemical problem. Thus, when we applied crank case ventilation the lessening of repair bills resulted in maintenance economies and there was a further saving in oil. Before crank case ventilation, manufacturers recommended drainage of oil every 500 miles. Today you drain oil at 2,000 miles. Your cost for oil has been reduced as from four to one.

The work we have done and are doing in lubrication research is done in co-operation with the oil in-dustry which is benefited because vastly more people buy oil for automobiles when the cost and waste are lessened. This saving and almost countless others add up to one thing—millions operate automobiles today who otherwise could not afford to do so. Year by year the industry has been working intensively to make it possible for more people to enjoy automobiles and to use them more generously.

Anywhere you choose to put your finger on an automobile, I can show you a whole series of im-provements. Who that was driving automobiles fif-teen years ago does not remember the inconvenience caused by the breaking of a fan belt? In those days this belt had nothing to do but fan a current of air across the radiator in the cooling system. It didn't run a water pump or a generator or anything else. Yet it was unreliable. A few thousand miles was the maxi-mum life. We decided to increase the life of a fan belt. The first thing done was to develop a testing de-vice that would tell us accurately how long a fan belt lasted, and if possible what made it break. We got fan belts from all the manufacturers. Some of the original specimens lasted only four or five hours on this testing machine, but after a couple of years of research and experimenting, we began to develop fan belts that would last for several thousand hours. Today fan belt trouble has been eliminated almost entirely from motorcar operations, and yet they do a great deal more work. A small research job, you might say, yet it involved the expenditure of perhaps a couple of hundred thousand dollars. Research is expensive. There are hundreds of failures for every achievement.

We have tackled so many of these kinds of problems I can't begin to remember all of them. Here is just one more that is most important. As speeds increase, balance becomes exceedingly important. Lack of balance anywhere in a mechanism causes vibration. Vibration is detrimental to the life of the mechanism, but more important, the rider is made uncomfortable. We found we had to balance all moving parts, especially crank shafts, very accurately. Yet there weren't any machines available to do this on a production basis. So General Motors developed a balancing machine that does a very difficult job in a thoroughly scientific manner. It shows just where metal must be removed to afford perfect balance. This machine, wonderfully intricate, is so simple in operation that an unskilled operator by watching a wave of light until it forms a straight line can do the trick. Most of the industry today uses our balancing machines. They are used also by airplane manufacturers and by the manufacturers of all manner of revolving machinery.

One day we went over to the research division seeking Mr. Kettering. I wanted to talk to him about the Diesel engine. I had been wondering why it was that, notwithstanding the higher efficiency of the Diesel in turning heat units in the fuel into power, that type of power unit had made relatively so little progress. I said to him, "Why is it, Ket, that the Diesel never seems to get anywhere?"

"That is an easy one: Because engineers insist on making it so it cannot work effectively."

I made an agreement with him right there. I was to buy the best available business then making Diesels, so we could most quickly achieve contact with the practical side of current practice, and Ket was to determine how the engine ought to be made. A simple approach, to be sure, but see what happens. A more effective type of engine power in relation to weight opened up possibilities that before had been impractical. Ten miles outside of Chicago now is a $25,-000,000 plant equipped to make Diesel electric locomotives from beginning to end. The latest technique in production, the resources to build a quantity at a time, irrespective of the flow of orders, is continually bringing down the cost and expanding the economies and other advantages of that type of motive power. What does that mean to you? It has reduced the time of travel by rail from Chicago to the West Coast from

55 or 60 hours to 39¾ hours—two nights and one day. But that is by no means all. As applied to the undramatic but essential duty of a switching engine, it is possible for a railroad to buy a Diesel electric switcher, discard the steam locomotive, and pay the entire cost of the Diesel electric job, including the carrying charges, with the out-of-pocket savings of the Diesel electric engine as against the steam one. Yet some political leaders have tried to tell us the world is finished, that there is no chance to invest our savings in new enterprise. I say, without reservation, that efficient as the American producing plant is in a relative sense, it is obsolete in terms of today's technology. There exists the most wonderful opportunity to rebuild America with the tools of today. Billions of dollars are needed. Millions of work hours are involved; the burden of unemployment ceases to exist. Better goods and services result in lower costs and more favorable selling prices.

We will sit around the conference table in General Motors and talk for hours about the influence of a dollar on the cost of a car. We know every dollar added to the cost means more than a dollar added to the consumer price. We know a higher consumer price means fewer consumer sales. When we find we can soundly reduce the price we are happy. We know it means more business. When we must increase the price we are worried. We know it means less business. We spend millions of dollars annually for better equipment to save relatively little on the cost of the car. If through better engineering we can cut the cost fifty cents we consider it an achievement because we know everybody gains.

The sum of this thinking and approach to the problem of design and manufacture is expressed in the wonderful values represented in the motorcar of today. But see what is happening: when through research, or engineering or some phase of our production we proudly save fifty cents, some taxing authority comes along and adds $25, and sometimes specifies it must be added in such a way the customer can't find out; and $25 is a small part of the total tax cost added to the motorcar during the past few years. Apparently the taxation, quite apart from defense requirements, is just starting, too. The consumer must pay, but everyone pays in a lower standard of living, unemployment with general deterioration of the social and economic structure. What the end is to be I do not know, but I do know that notwithstanding all the wonders we are accomplishing in technological progress, we just can't keep up with the politicians' ability to spend our money. Even the scientific approach seems futile in the face of this problem.

PART VI

Adventures Ahead

THESE adventures of mine in the world of industry constitute a story not perhaps greatly different, except in detail, than could be told by many others who have contributed to a greater or less degree in the up-building of the American system of enterprise to its present high level of effectiveness. We can all appreciate another's devotion to the various interests that go to absorb our daily lives, that add to the pleasure of living and especially those that serve to lend a helping hand to others less fortunate in life's great adventure. We even listen with patience to the other fellow's achievement on the golf course even if in that case we feel, as I do sometimes, sorry for so much energy and ambition directed into such unprofitable channels. All this is recognized as both a necessary and a desirable part of our scheme of life.

On the other hand, when that interest takes the form of devotion to a business, then somehow or other these rules do not so universally apply. And that is particularly true today. Too many ascribe such interest to the desire for material wealth and that only. Too many who would not think of a material motive in any one of many other activities I might mention, cannot seem to realize that the greatest real thrill that life offers is to create, to construct, to develop something useful, to overcome the obstacles and difficulties that continually impede the road to progress. Devotion to such a cause can be just as altruistic as devotion to any of our other interests and ambitions, and superimposed upon such a satisfaction is the thought that one is making a contribution toward advancing both the social and economic status of the community.

The ambition, the willingness to make the sacrifice to rank high in the world of material accomplishments, is not only a highly worthy objective, but the fact that it has until recently been so regarded undoubtedly has been an important contributing factor in the development of America and of the highest standard of living anywhere existing. The profit motive is an essential component in the capitalistic system, but it is far from the sole influence as an actuating force as applied to the individual in contributing to the world's great accomplishments. Beyond a certain point soon reached the sole urge is for still greater success, a recognition of one's ability to accomplish, and the satisfaction that results from it all. The anxieties, the responsibilities, the necessity of living the life of the cause rather than one's own life could not possibly be compensated for in any material way. These are my conclusions as I have watched American business and those associated with it, in a very broad way, over many years. It applies just as truly to those comprising the General Motors organization. I know it has importantly contributed to our success.

A newspaper commentator recently wrote in relation to some testimony I had given before a Congressional Committee that I was proud of my figures and had reason to be. He was both right and wrong. I am proud of General Motors figures, but only because they present the most practical method of dealing with General Motors accomplishments—these are really what I am proud of. I am obliged to be statistical. During the twenty years which ended at New Year's Day, 1940, General Motors created new products measured at $18,929,727,535. These were the total net sales. But the performance becomes more representative if limited to the years in which the organization really commenced to develop effectiveness. From 1927 to the end of 1939 total sales amounted to

$14,535,420,620. In this period there was reinvested in the business to make more work and to create still more wealth in the future and do it with greater efficiency, $397,842,840. The stockholders, who increased in number from 66,000 to nearly 400,000, received as dividends $1,675,762,009. An average total of 193,000 employes shared a total payroll distribution of $4,010,749,826. A considerable proportion of other billions spent for materials and freight also went to workers in other lines of endeavor: on railroads, in cotton fields, mines, ships, in fact, everywhere. Moreover, several of these thirteen years were the worst in our economic history. Yet in no year, even during the depression, did General Motors fail to make a profit or fail to pay a dividend to its stockholders, both common and preferred.

Economic disturbance means human beings in trouble. And there was trouble in Detroit in the early part of 1933. In fact, the whole state of Michigan was in trouble. I was called on the telephone one night by the President and asked to take breakfast with him on the following morning. Arriving, I found my friend Walter P. Chrysler and one or two officials of the Treasury Department already there. The problem was the condition of the banks in Detroit. Unless help could be obtained it was unlikely they could open after the Lincoln's Birthday holiday.

Chrysler and myself were asked to see what we could do to lend a helping hand in the emergency. Day and night conferences resulted in the unfolding of a condition that was far too big for any or all of us to handle. Conditions were very serious. Still we were powerless. All financial institutions in the state of Michigan were closed on February 14, 1933, on the order of the governor. And the two principal banks of Detroit did not again open and were later liquidated. Within that state at that time were concentrated our major manufacturing facilities. The savings of our employes were impounded. We had on deposit in Michigan approximately $18,800,000. We needed cash in many cities in the state to pay our workers, and to conduct our business.

Just think, here was a city of about one and one half million people. All their cash resources were impounded. Things were so demoralized that everyone's credit was subject to question. At Detroit's leading business club you had to pay cash in advance for your luncheon. It had been my practice to spend the greater part of every other week in Detroit and as the weeks passed I could see the deterioration of the city's business activities. Something had to be done to release at least part of the funds tied up and to give the city some semblance of banking facilities or absolute chaos soon would result.

Conferences were continually being held between officials of the United States Treasury Department and the state of Michigan, also with the officers of the closed banks and the leading citizens of the city, in the attempt to find some practical way out of the difficulty. In these conferences General Motors participated through the able advice of Donaldson Brown, now vice chairman of General Motors, and of John Thomas Smith, vice-president and general counsel. Finally it became obvious that the situation required that some strong organization, capable within itself of assuming the responsibility of affording the essential relief, should step forward. Otherwise exceedingly serious developments could be expected: people were suffering. It was not a problem of selection. General Motors was the only organization that had the resources to do the job and General Motors did it.

With the Reconstruction Finance Corporation we set up a new bank in Detroit with a capital of $25,000,000: half was subscribed by the Reconstruction Finance Corporation, which took preferred stock in the new bank. General Motors put up the other half. This $12,500,000 was an underwriting of the bank's common stock. As a result the National Bank of Detroit was opened on March 24, 1933, a bank with new personnel. It was completely liquid and in every way a Godsend to the people of Detroit in an hour of real need. Today this bank is the dominant financial institution of Detroit and one of the larger banks of the country.

It is easy now to tell the story of this $12,500,000 banking investment, but it was not so easy a matter to assume such a responsibility and to decide to make an investment of that size in such uncertain times as then existed—times impossible to appreciate fully in the different atmosphere of today. It has turned out to be a profitable investment for General Motors, but it must be evident as I tell the story that here the profit motive had no direct part: as a matter of fact, nobody was thinking of profits, but rather how to save what they could. The objective at that time was to perform a service to the community of which General Motors was, of course, an important part, but after all a relatively small proportion of the total.

Shortly after the new bank was opened, General Motors made a public offer to the people of Detroit to sell all the stock the community would buy at the same price it had paid, but very little was taken. People were not looking for bank stocks as an investment in those times. I have already discussed the subject of industrial bigness and outlined its importance in an economic sense and in doing so emphasized the necessity of industrial management recognizing its broader relationship to the public interest in the conduct of its affairs. This story of the National Bank of Detroit illustrates the concept of the General Motors management as to that phase of its responsibility—its duty to the community and to the economy as a whole.

The bank episode we have been talking about was, of course, only one phase of the depression and its impact on General Motors. In the year 1933, the automobile industry lost 75 per cent of its 1929 volume. Naturally, we had to curtail; expenses had to be reduced in accordance with such a tremendous shrinkage of income. General Motors believes in balancing its budget on the right side if possible, but balancing it in any event. Industry is not like government. It can't pass on deficits year after year to its stockholders without such action leading to embarrassing questions, and ultimately management loses its job—all as it should be. For some reason or other—I cannot understand why—taxpayers, and many are also stockholders, will stand for exorbitant government expenditures with huge deficits year after year and apparently like it. "The bigger the better" appears to be the approach. Perhaps the reason is that they can't see that they pay the bill. They don't seem to realize that they always pay in higher prices or reduced income, in fact usually both. Perhaps some day they will learn. Let us hope so.

Celebrating General Motors' 25,000,000th car. Between Sloan and Knudsen is Charles H. Blades, oldest in the industry. At 80 he still works in the Olds plant. He hammered out the front axle of the first commercially successful car in America.

Mr. Sloan and William S. Knudsen greeted by a group of General Motors workmen at one of the plants in Southern California.

But, notwithstanding our curtailed income, we continued without reduction both our research and engineering activities. Every year of the depression we spent millions of dollars in new tools and new machinery to make possible new and better models. And we were able to increase the value of the consumer's dollars because material was cheaper and labor both cheaper and more efficient. In that way we stimulated what buying power was available, hence providing all the employment we could.

Many may wonder why the automobile industry brings out a new model every year. The reason is simple. We want to make available to you, as rapidly as we can, the most advanced knowledge and practice in the building of motorcars; we want to make you dissatisfied with your current car so you will buy a new one—you who can afford it. In General Motors we have been spending yearly about $35,000,000 for this purpose partly in new machinery and partly in special tools. And you who can afford it perform—probably unconsciously—a very important economic service. You pass on to the used-car market your old car at a value in transportation with which no new car could possibly compete. Eventually your old car may be sold to somebody at $50 or even less and that somebody gets transportation at a price that would be impossible any other way. Thus the utility of the

[*177*]

motorcar is expanded and made available to millions who would otherwise be deprived of its benefits and pleasures. But that is not all. The automobile industry is able to expand its own payrolls and those of others through the production incident to the glamour of the new model. We frequently hear that the used-car problem is the curse of the automobile industry. That is in a way true but it is a blessing in another and in a broader and bigger way.

It was at the beginning of the depression that we entered the Diesel engine field. I have already told the story how through the application of this type of prime mover in more effective form, we have, I believe I am safe in saying, obsoleted America's railway motive power and made a real contribution in many other fields where power is used. Take a ride in one of the modern streamliners and see if you do not agree, and the railroad companies' books tell a similar story.

This was by no means an easy accomplishment. In some respects it was a research project. The heart of the problem was the injector through which the fuel has to be atomized before it passes into the Diesel cylinder. With all his devotion to precision work old Henry Leland would have said our research men were trying to do the impossible. To bore the nearly invisible holes called for by the scientific principle that had been established, we had to make a drill as fine as a mosquito's bill. You can scarcely see it with your naked eye, yet it cuts through steel. This was accomplished by a group of men trained in various branches of science. Working with ample scientific resources they produced a result seemingly impossible. To-day the two-cycle Diesel is creating, not alone more power, but more employment, wherever it is used.

The depression era saw the beginning of the air-conditioning industry. For generations men have dreamed of achieving control of the atmosphere in which we work, play and rest when indoors. Today almost anyone can have or enjoy the use of a motor-car. The time is fast approaching when almost anyone will be able to sleep and work in air-conditioned rooms. Tomorrow when you buy your new car do not be surprised if you are asked whether you wish to have it air conditioned. That is right now in the realm of the possible, even if still a while off.

I have told the story of "Frigidaire" and the electric refrigerator but there is one phase of its technical evolution that is worth while relating, particularly as it illustrates the varied problems that face research in our large industrial organizations. In the earlier days the gas used as a refrigerant was a hazard—so much so that refrigeration was barred from use in certain places. But the limitations of this gas became very important when it was used in air-conditioning units, where in case of accident its toxic qualities might prove injurious to human life. Again a research problem arose. What could be done?

The heart of the problem was in chemistry. The use of sulphur dioxide, ammonia, carbon dioxide or methyl chloride involved hazards. A better refrigerant was a necessity for air-conditioning units. Thomas Midgely, Jr., who played an important role as an associate of Mr. Kettering in the development of Ethyl gas, got the assignment. Soon he had need of a specialist who could not be found in America, but one who had the foremost knowledge of a chemical substance called fluorine. A Belgian chemist, Dr. A. L. Henne, was induced to come and help. Thereafter there was developed a compound of carbon, chlorine and fluorine called dichlerodifluoromethane, a clear white liquid that boils at twenty-one degrees below zero! In fact a whole series of synthetic refrigerants was developed. Today, under the general trade name Freon, this fluid is used generally in air conditioning and in most domestic refrigerators now being manufactured. It is practically odorless, non-irritating, non-explosive, non-toxic, non-corrosive, and non-injurious to foods, flowers, furs and fabrics. "Freon" means that people who dwell in the tropics can live as comfortably, work as energetically as residents of New England. Research has eliminated the limitations. Mechanical refrigeration and air conditioning are now without technical restriction as to their availability.

These are only incidental illustrations, important as they nevertheless are, of how during an era of industrial and economic stagnation work was going on in industry's workshops and laboratories in the way of creating new approaches to better living, more opportunities for employment and developing for the future additional needs for the constructive use of our savings in profitable enterprise. Out of the brains in various General Motors divisions came projects for new vacuum cleaners, automobile radios, electric ranges, heating plants and other useful things to make possible this better living. We know, of course, that unless we can produce better appliances we not only cannot hope to sell them, but we are not contributing anything in the way of progress. At Bristol, Conn., engineers of New Departure Division invented a two-speed bicycle with a front-wheel brake. Two speeds enable a rider to "get away" quicker, to climb hills with less effort and go faster on the level, somewhat analogous to the gear shift in the automobile. Despite automobiles, bicycles still find a market. New Departure is a big factor in the field; it makes about 950,000 coaster brakes and 1,100,000 bicycle wheel hubs a year, as well as from 35,000,000 to 40,000,000 ballbearings a year.

A few years ago we decided we should try to make a contribution in the form of a better engineering technique in the home-appliance field—such as washers and ironers. It was becoming essential in the distribution of Frigidaire to provide a complete General Motors line. One day a man came who had a basic idea to make a new kind of washer. Certain disadvantages had caused others to reject his invention. Our engineers were able to overcome those disadvantages. By embodying his idea with our development, we will be able to produce in the near future a fully automatic cycle washer with an improved washing action that fully protects the most delicate fabrics. After it has been charged with soiled garments and started, timing devices control its actions. When the washer stops automatically the clothes have been washed, rinsed, treated with bluing and damp dried. Thus, in two years, thanks to the availability of ample resources of capital and ability, this inventor's work reaches a wide market.

Competition and progress are inseparable. Thirty years ago, when the industry was telling its customers they could have a car of any color "so long as it's black," the intention was to increase volume through simplification of manufacturing detail. Make them run. Get the price down. People wanted cars! That was all that then mattered. Today for exactly the same reason—to get volume—the customer can, over a wide range, really have his car any color he desires and trimmed with any material he fancies. In mass production there has been developed such amazing flexibility that it may well be said that every car in certain particulars could be a custom job.

In 1927 Cadillac caused a tremendous commotion with an announcement to the effect that customers might have a choice of 500 color and upholstery options. Today there are about a million possible options. For example, you can have an Oldsmobile with or without Hydra-Matic drive, with six or eight cylinders, any one of a dozen body styles, choice of fifteen kinds of interior trim, any one of twenty colors over-all, or different on the wheels, with or without radio, heater and so on. At our plant in Linden, New Jersey, the multiplicity of styles and colors revealed as ticketed parts flow together at the assembly line with a permissible error in timing of only a few seconds— not minutes—is astonishing. Visitors whose understanding of the process has not advanced beyond the "any-color-you-like-so-long-as-it's-black" stage are further bewildered as they observe the variety of the production to discover eleven kinds of chassis taking final shape as Oldsmobiles, Pontiacs and Buicks. And all this happens on the same assembly line continuously moving!

This is the answer to a question frequently asked—Why does not General Motors make cars for stock in those periods of the year when consumer buying is at a minimum? We do in a degree. Standard combinations of colors and trim permit a floating supply in the hands of our dealers. But to sell all possible, we make cars "to order" to please individual taste; by doing so we create additional business, even though it entails more work. The schedules must provide for the flow of the right part of the right color to the right point in the assembly line at the right time. To lose the sequence of parts and colors might involve stopping the assembly line, and that is a crime in the manufacture of automobiles.

Style is what I have just been talking about—eye appeal as applied to the motorcar. In the old Hyatt days, as I journeyed from one engineering department to another in my efforts to sell my bearings, I used to wonder why more attention was not given to appearance. The engineer was both the technician and the artist. Engineering deals with the realities. Engineers must be practical but they do not necessarily have to have an artist's conception nor recognize the importance of appearance in the sales scheme of things, especially today. In my dreams of what might be done I visualized an organized effort to promote the maximum in eye appeal—a styling approach separate from the usual engineering approach. In these early days French motorcars, like everything French, were looked upon as leaders from the standpoint of styling. Well, I would obtain the best talent that France could provide. I would create a styling staff and provide it with every facility to develop the attractive. This, like many other dreams, was all brought about in due course of time. Today the appearance of a motorcar is a most important factor in the selling end of the business—perhaps the most important single factor because everybody knows that all cars will run. One part of my dream, however, did not develop in the way I had anticipated. We were able to develop such superior talent right here at home that, just as in engineering prestige, American cars advanced in styling prestige to the point that even in France, the style creator of the world, American cars became the smart thing to own. Today our Styling Section has representatives in all our foreign manufacturing plants. Detroit sets the world's pace in motorcar styling.

Year by year industrial progress has been defending employment and increasing it. In 1910, when closed bodies became available for volume production, the use of motorcars was extended throughout the entire year. In 1911 when Kettering brought his first self-starter from a barn workshop to Henry Leland he immediately increased the potential market; henceforth, women too could drive. In 1915 tilt beam headlights added the night hours to the motorcar's field of usefulness. Four-wheel brakes brought increased safety of operation—and a wider market—in 1923. In 1924 Duco lacquer finishes lowered maintenance costs for car owners and importantly increased our ability to reduce production costs. In 1932 "super safe" headlights were applied as one of a series of improvements designed to eliminate driving hazards. There was Fisher "No Draft" ventilation in 1933; "Knee-Action" in 1934; "Turret Top" bodies in 1935; automatic transmissions in 1937; steering column gear shift control in 1938; and many others. Each marks an advance in the continuous effort to perfect the automobile. Each helps to sell cars by making them both more useful and more attractive and each additional car means additional work—more national wealth. These are only a part of the scores of developments. The remarkable thing even to one like myself who has had a most intimate part in this evolution of technological progress is the fact that, adding, as these improvements have, many man hours of employment in the construction of each motorcar and notwithstanding that the hourly wage rate has nearly doubled, selling prices have not gone up but down. The explanation is found in more intensive engineering and more effective use of materials and labor, together with the technological advancement in production processes. That is the important part of a remarkable achievement.

Things are never changed on General Motors cars for the sake of change. They are changed only in the belief they can be genuinely improved in some way that will increase their appeal to the public taste and at the same time keep faith with the obligations of mass selling imposed by mass production.

Through science we have largely eliminated noise; the last big step in this field was the intake silencer, announced in 1930. You will see any time you lift the engine hood what looks like a black can placed up over the carburetor. Do you realize what an ingenious instrument it is? If you can think back to the car you drove prior to 1930 you may remember that stepping on its accelerator brought forth a roar which you thought of as power. It was simply "roar." But in 1930 a sixteen cylinder Cadillac was developed so silent you had the feeling of coasting even at sixty miles an hour. Fewer than 400 of those Cadillacs were made in a year but now all the millions of new automobiles each has its "intake silencer."

In developing this invention the sound frequencies of the old engine "roar" were calculated. Then the silencer was designed so that the volume of air rushing through it made a noise neutralizing the noise of the intake as the engine cylinders sucked in air. That "can" contains a series of chambers or pipes. It is a pipe organ that makes a noise to kill another noise. On a few Cadillacs it was expensive; on all the millions of automobiles its unit cost is a few cents—far below its value to the car user who may now hear symphonic music from his radio, or Amos 'n Andy, instead of engine roar as he rides.

Your automobile is ingeniously packed with instruments which are expressions of just about everything known in chemistry and physics. It is the one thing in common use that uses so much scientific fact.

Unless we had engineered a way to make intake silencers more cheaply most car engines would still be roaring. But obviously even with our highly developed mechanical processes, far more workers are required to produce millions of intake silencers every year than if they were made by the dozen by hand labor.

Earlier in this story I told about recognizing the necessity of building General Motors engineering staffs and research to the highest standard that the best brains and finest facilities would make possible. Even so I recognized that constructive ideas would develop from without as well as from within, so I established the New Devices Section as an organized effort to encourage outsiders having ideas to submit them to us for examination and appraisal. Thousands of ideas and devices are examined very thoroughly every year, but although it does not seem as if it ought to be so, the facts are that there are only a few per year which are of real interest to us. And yet an examination of the records proves conclusively that we have not overlooked much of real value. I am inclined to think the answer lies in the fact that industry's technical position is now so far advanced that future developments are likely to be largely restricted to the more highly organized research and engineering activities like our own. There will be exceptions of course. If my assumption is correct, the importance of encouraging the broadest possible expansion of such work as an essential in industry's scheme of things and as a means of insuring progress becomes more and more evident. Research, using that term in the broad sense and applying it to all functional activity, can be the best investment any industrial organization makes.

About 1926 a lanky fellow walked in with a model of an invention he said would enable any driver to shift gears without clashing. Shifting was then difficult! Somewhat of an art in a way. None of us had ever seen or heard of him before. But we welcomed his idea. Here was an exception.

Several years later, after constant collaboration between the inventor and our engineers, his invention was applied to the Cadillac transmission. It was still too expensive and complicated to justify application to the lower-price cars. But finally Chevrolet was changed to the synchro-mesh type of transmission, and the days of clashing gears were gone forever. What made it possible? Lowering of the unit cost!

Sometimes we add some improvement to a line of our more expensive cars, thinking its cost as applied to the lower-price lines makes it prohibitive, yet sooner or later and very soon in most cases the skill of our engineering staff and the ability of our manufacturing people bring the cost down to the point where the benefits can be extended to all, irrespective of the price they pay.

Next, this same inventor, after more than fourteen years of intensive engineering contact with the transmission field, produced an idea well in advance of his own synchro-mesh. It is really an entirely automatic transmission and, in connection with a fluid fly wheel, which in itself is an old device, entirely eliminates the clutch. It is operated by hydraulic controls. An expert looking at it seems to see a mechanical ghost of the planetary transmission of the old Ford Model T. It is possible today only because of the use of new and superior materials now available.

It is the continual demonstration of the power of engineers to find in science constant means of improving automobiles, which justifies the prediction that as today's low-priced Chevrolet is a better value in almost every way than 1930's Cadillac, so the cars of 1950 will outclass the best we can offer in 1940.

As I say this I recall how often I have asked myself as I watched the following year's models through their various stages of development: How can we possibly make them better next time? But we always do and I have come to recognize that we always can just so long as we are willing to pay the price which progress always exacts. That price is not in money alone— that is the easiest part—but in skill as measured by experience and ability, in imagination that visualizes what might be possible and—let us not forget—in long hours of hard work and many discouragements to be overcome. Those are the factors which determine the progress of the future, not only of General Motors but of each of us severally and of all of us collectively. There are no short cuts no matter who does the planning.

There was one exhibit in particular in the General Motors Building at the New York World's Fair which I sincerely wish every man, woman and child in the United States had seen and understood, and the lesson to be learned is not a difficult one. I wish everyone, everywhere, could have the opportunity to ponder long and hard over this exhibit so that there could be developed a wider understanding of a few of the simple truths that govern industry's processes, that particularly affect employment and that influence the lives and future of every one of us.

The exhibit consisted of two motorcars, one of 1913, the other of 1940. There were tens of thousands of the 1913 car sold in that year at $1,125. And there were likewise tens of thousands of the 1940 model sold for $800. The consumer paid at the rate of $.50 per pound for the former and paid $.26 per pound for the latter. Of course, actually we cannot compare these cars pound for pound because the 1940 car was so superior to its ancestor in quality, appointments and equipment. This is why the 1940 car absorbed as many hours of employment as the car of 1913. It represented vastly greater value, yet it sold for a third less. In the intervening years, through the capitalization of technological improvement and through better managerial technique, we have been able so to increase our efficiency that the productivity of each worker has been enormously expanded. That and only that is what makes all this possible.

What has this increased ability to produce meant to wage earners? The average hourly wage of the automotive worker then was 30 cents. Today it is 98 cents. I have already made the observation that, in the long run, the wage rate depends solely on the pro-

On the final assembly line. 1941 Chevrolets.

Three American automobile makers of Detroit.

ductivity of the worker. There was in this exhibit a formula which our political friends do not understand —the pity of it. That formula is: We must pay higher wages to stimulate purchasing power. We must reduce prices to stimulate consumption. These things can only be accomplished through technological improvement. And it is through this process that we can increase employment. Let us encourage it! If this process of development is permitted to continue, there can be no question of our ability as a people to create a better life for everybody.

Today it is clear that every man, woman and child, including generations yet to be born, has a stake in the power of General Motors and of similar units in industry to function, and not only that, but to function efficiently. Every thinking person realizes today as never before that industrial power is national power. What then is General Motors?

Is it plants and machines? Is it the hundreds of thousands of stockholders? Is it the few at the top? Is it 220,000 workers on its pay rolls? For me the essential ingredient—the heart, if you please—of our organization is a group of not more than 10,000 workers whose skill in management, in engineering and in science as well as in the special crafts makes possible the work in which all the others are engaged. Were all the plants to be destroyed in some manner, given time and capital, with those 10,000 men the business could be reconstituted.

I want to repeat and to emphasize the fact that the industrial strength of the United States, greatly enhanced since the last war, has been menaced by unsound national economic policies and destructive propaganda of many kinds tending to create uncertainty as to the future of the American system of enterprise.

In America industrial organizations, under normal conditions, are only incidentally a source of production for military purposes. They are the best institutions ever developed for saving humanity from poverty. In recent years some have lost sight of these facts.

When I first attended a world's fair I began to realize that science applied to industry portended the abolition of poverty. I was a young man when I saw the World's Columbian Exposition. Now, with the marvelous panorama the New York World's Fair offered, I can see that in the intervening years we have learned how to produce enough of everything necessary for a comfortable existence and we have hardly started. In 1893 only the rich could afford carriages. But no one was rich enough to have an automobile. Now, automobiles are available to practically everyone. And establishments for the co-operation of labor, capital, and science such as our successful industrial organizations, are the most significant economic development of the passing years. They have no precedent in history. They have made it all possible.

As Charles F. Kettering says, "Too many of us are clustered around the power house." But we are not obliged to continue this congestion. Here is where industry has a marvelous opportunity to attune its operations more effectively to the needs of the community as a whole. Just think, there are 3,070 counties in the United States, but crowded into a mere eight counties are the people and plants that produce one quarter of all the manufactured wealth. These counties are better known by the names of the cities that spread over them: Chicago, Detroit, New York, Philadelphia, Los Angeles, Pittsburgh, Cleveland, Buffalo. In 1937 the total value of goods manufactured in those counties was $15,350,767,000! A lot of jobs are represented.

A change is visible. For a number of years a considerable migration of industry has been in progress. A part of the cotton textile manufacturing industry has gone into the Southeastern states. There has been a great increase in iron and steel production in the Southeast. In other directions there is a tendency away from congested areas.

There is a sound fundamental lesson to be learned. The cost of living is less in the smaller community. The same wage rate means a higher standard of living—and conversely—an equivalent standard of living means lower costs and lower selling prices. That is the real approach, because production is expanded—more employment, more wealth, is created—more things for more people in more places.

Our relief problems could never be so serious if more factory work were distributed among people in the smaller communities who could live on small subsistence farms. After all, a home of one's own is an aspiration seemingly common to all. The more home owners, the more of our people have a real stake in the nation's welfare; and relatively more homes are possible in small communities than in our congested urban centers. People in cities dream of security as something to be found in the country. But it was the drudgery and hardships of living, as well as lack of money-producing employment, that drove people into the cities. Well, now we have cures for such dissatisfactions. Science and industry have changed all that. The disadvantages of small community life have vanished. Into smaller communities should go some of those jobs now centered in big cities. Without any increase in dollar wages such a shift of industrial activity would bring to the mass of wage earners a wonderful increase in real wages.

General Motors is striving for decentralization of its plants and has been working in that direction for many years. As a matter of policy, in the last four or five years we have established units in fifteen or twenty smaller places. One difficulty is that our average unit is large. If there are 5,000 workers, with their families they number perhaps 20,000 people. That means that the grocery stores, barber shops, banks, bakeries, movies, etc. which thrive on their business, add many more to the community, so even with General Motors as the sole employer, the community begins to expand rapidly in size.

But there is one mistake we must not and need not make. We need not carry decentralization of industry to the point where it increases our costs and selling prices. I say need not because all the economic forces are toward lower costs. But we must keep certain limitations in mind.

Another epic American migration. That is what I mean by decentralization. I would expect as this vision took shape to see as an actual movement countless families regrouping themselves for a life more secure and far richer in its prospects for happiness. Each family would be traveling to a home of its own in a community organized to provide every service of

[*197*]

civilized society. Jobs for the wage earners of the families would be provided in a factory unit representing each community's gain through industrial decentralization.

The houses would be pre-fabricated. They would be more enduring, better designed, more comfortable than any with which people are now familiar and the cost of such a house of five rooms should not be far from $2,500. This would include an automatic, modern heating plant, an automatic refrigerator, an electric stove, an electric washing machine, an electric dish washer and perhaps even air conditioning.

In General Motors Corporation we have recognized for many years the opportunity represented by housing. It could well be the greatest industrial opportunity since the development of the automobile began.

Sometime ago we calculated what it would cost to build a Chevrolet such as sells F.O.B. Detroit for $800 were we to use the hand tools and the methods commonly employed in house building. This is one for Ripley! A hand-made Chevrolet would cost not less than $5,000 and it couldn't be nearly so good a car! Now ask that question in reverse: How cheaply could a house be produced by factory methods, on a mass-production basis?

Why doesn't somebody do something? I believe General Motors could do the job effectively. It would take time—five years, at least—to show a reasonably effective result. It has been suggested that we tackle the problem. It would be a tremendous undertaking involving great hazards, a heavy responsibility and many disappointments. It must be clear that the political economic situation in its relationship to industry, as it exists today, to say nothing of the attacks that might be expected if we were to develop in such an entirely different field of enterprise, would preclude any serious consideration of such a possibility. But that is not all. The political power of the pressure groups that would be antagonized by such a revolutionary approach to one of our greatest industries might well make any organization hesitate, and justly so.

Industry can, and I hope will, solve the housing problem but it will take large resources, great courage, and ability of the highest order to put the job across in a big way.

After all, the housing problem would appear to be relatively simple as compared to the transportation problem which faced the people who built this country. Industry has solved that problem in an amazing way with trains, ships, automobiles and airplanes— highly technical achievements. Industry has solved a great many other great problems:—communications, illumination, power. I believe it is safe to say that homes for the lowest-income group lag far behind the standard of our other achievements.

We have seen earlier in this story how the continuously increasing demand for more and always more cars led to the building of more and more, just as the demand for better and better cars resulted in a continuous series of engineering improvements. In natural evolution as the years passed, the demand took the form of more and more orders to keep pace with the constantly increasing production, and finally the cry became: "Too many cars—too few orders." Overproduction was threatened, in other words.

Large territories originally in the hands of big distributors were broken down into smaller areas for more intensive cultivation of the market. Many of these large distributors in the earlier years made fortunes, especially when they were lucky enough to have picked out a popular make. The industry now was turning its attention aggressively to the problem of sales—advertising and distribution. The pace became hotter and hotter. More and more cars meant more and more orders and more and more dealers to get the orders. Finally not only too many cars but too many dealers.

Much of the impact of this intensive and constantly increasing competition fell on the dealers who sold the cars at retail. Still the retail business continued to be profitable. That was the answer for a while. But rapidly increasing volume in the prosperous days of the latter half of the twenties served to obscure the fact that the economic strength of the retail end of the business was being sapped by the constantly increasing competition. This situation was aggravated by the development of the used-car problem. To sell a new car meant to take a used car in trade and at an allowance in excess of its real value. Anything to effect a sale. Dealer dollar volume was increasing but dealer dollar profits were decreasing.

I realized that the big problem of the product—engineering and manufacturing—was becoming secondary and was being outranked by an equally big job of injecting into the distribution end of our business the scientific approach. I saw that as all cars approached a more common level of usefulness the strength of the distribution system would be the most important factor in the competitive race. Markets must be defined and protected. Enough dealers of the right size to deliver the potential of those markets and no more. Production must be determined by retail sales—no longer by the ambition for big figures and statistics must be made available to chart the course. We had to get the facts and act accordingly. This we did in a very comprehensive way.

Stocks of new cars as well as of used cars in dealers'

hands were reported tri-monthly. Dealer accounting was inaugurated. More important still, I instituted a plan of Dealer Councils by which representative groups of dealers from every section of the country were brought three times a year around a conference table with General Motors executives for the discussion of mutual problems. These and many other developments are all parts of the elaborate system of fact-finding that now prevails and which guides us in determining the administration of distribution and its underlying fundamental policies. Today, distribution in General Motors is a science. General Motors regards its dealers as partners in its business. It recognizes the vital importance of a dealer profit and of dealer security, for upon these depend the value of a General Motors franchise. Great progress has been made. Much more is needed, for we aspire to only the highest standards in General Motors. But suffice it to say, today the profit opportunities of a motorcar merchant holding a General Motors franchise will challenge the ambition of the most intelligent and aggressive. I take this opportunity of paying tribute to the many thousands of able and hard-working dealers associated with us in the great General Motors enterprise. They have done and are doing their part, and I appreciate it.

I wish I might tell fully the story of the development of the overseas markets—how we have carried the General Motors flag and American industry into every country where roads exist. It is an exciting story of a really splendid accomplishment amid great difficulties, especially in recent years. Few realize the barriers that have developed, even before the present war, such as embargoes, limitations on exchange, nationalism, quotas, cartels—all restricting the movement of international commerce. Many important automotive markets are already gone for the American manufacturer, others are on the way. The highly effective technique of the American system of mass production, together with our own highly efficient machinery, is being utilized more and more in other manufacturing countries. In view of the lower wages there prevailing, our competitive position is prejudiced, especially in the face of the growing economic restrictions.

Many years ago I recognized that it was impossible to assume that the more important manufacturing countries would continue to permit the exploitation of their markets from without, especially for such a vital need as motor transportation. Therefore, I moved toward complete manufacture in the more industrialized countries to the end that, while during recent years the position of the American industry in the overseas markets has been declining, General Motors has increased its share which in the latest normal year reached its highest point. These foreign designs do not compete with the domestic ones; rather they supplement them, more particularly in the non-manufacturing areas. The largest car produced in quantities overseas is smaller than the smallest car produced domestically. Because of the higher cost of production, the higher operating taxes for the owner, as well as the lower level of purchasing power existing in those countries, their people cannot afford the luxurious equipment of the American motorcar. There is food for much thinking in that simple fact.

The editor tells me my story is finished. Probably it should be. But it is difficult to compress within a few pages forty years' adventure in American enterprise, almost every day of which has had an interest all its own. But, after all, it is not of much importance what happened, or how it happened, but why. That is what counts. It is the lessons to be learned. Are they applicable along a broad front of industrial enterprise in the years to come? As my distinguished friend, Charles F. Kettering, tells us, the future is of consequence because there is where we are to spend the rest of our lives. General Motors started as an idea. It has become great as measured by almost any yardstick —technical achievement, earning power, wage rates, employment, contributions to human progress, opportunity. The conception of William C. Durant in the then little town of Flint, Michigan, in a relatively short space of time, developed into one of the greatest industrial enterprises of all time. That is the record. But again, why? Recognizing the essential opportunity, what are the underlying principles that have shown the way, and if the answer should be found in the story itself, then the story is well worth while. I believe that must be so because it is so essential a part of General Motors operating philosophy as to make it inseparable from General Motors itself. Here are those principles:

Management: The collective effort of intelligence, experience and imagination.

The facts: A constant search for the truth.

The open mind: Policy based upon analysis without prejudice.

Courage: The willingness to take a risk, recognizing the fact that leadership exacts a price.

Equity: Respect for the rights of others.

Confidence: The courage of one's convictions.

Loyalty: The willingness to make any sacrifice for the cause.

Progress: There must always be a better way.

And most important of all, for without it all else is of little avail: Work. The catalysis that energizes all these ingredients, so that they may take their respective parts in promoting the common cause.

Such are the basic principles that I laid down as my platform for the guidance of the organization at the time I became president of General Motors Corporation.

As the years have passed, they have been my constant guide. They have never failed in the many moments of stress and doubt. I am sure they will never fail any individual or any organization, irrespective of the problems that may arise, or the difficulties that must be faced.

Bill Knudsen and I were sitting in the Press Club of the General Motors Building at the New York World's Fair. We had just celebrated its opening. A thousand distinguished guests had seen the exhibit and had taken a ride through the Futurama. We had had dinner. A moving picture had been shown dramatizing the recent accomplishments of American industry in the form of new things—methods, processes and products. Every individual enterprise represented, and many others as well, had contributed to a symposium of progress. It was a stupendous record of accomplishment, especially in the face of a long period of depression. Everyone was electrified by what he had seen and heard. I realized that, in many ways, it was a new top in our evolution. Here were shown all our products, dressed in the very latest technological mode. A great array of devices dedicated to better living, making possible a wider horizon of contact and enjoyment.

"You know, Bill," I said to Mr. Knudsen, "all these products really tell the story of the American plan of free enterprise; the ceaseless research in the hope of producing more and better goods and services at ever greater values. They are symbolic of American industry today—the industrial scheme of things that is constantly turning luxuries into everyday conveniences for more people."

"And what we must never forget in this country," said Knudsen, "is that the only way to provide more jobs for people is to keep on doing the things that made all these things possible—only do them still better. Quality products, better methods, good wages, low prices, better tools, fair dealing. And," he added, "plenty of hard work from everybody."

"Just think, Bill," I said; "the wonder of it all is that we have only just begun. The opportunities for America are beyond the dreams of any man now alive, if we will only, through persistent work and enterprise, continue the pattern that was begun so long ago.

"Take the Futurama, for instance—a conception of what the world of 1960 may look like. But who knows what the world of 1960 really will be like? The real world of tomorrow will outstrip anything we can imagine today, if only we in this country will keep our vision and hold our faith in the fundamentals that make for progress.

"New comforts for the city, a new life for the country, conveniences in the home, progress in better living—new highways, new means of communication, strides in health and education and culture—the mind of man just cannot comprehend all the things that lie within our reach."

But back in my mind was another thought. It was this: *One thing sure: making tomorrow's dream come true will hold even greater adventures than those which began at the Hyatt plant over on the Harrison dump.*